Space

This volume is one of a series that examines
various aspects of computer technology and the
role computers play in modern life.

UNDERSTANDING COMPUTERS

Space

BY THE EDITORS OF TIME-LIFE BOOKS

TIME-LIFE BOOKS, ALEXANDRIA, VIRGINIA

Contents

The Leap Outward

"*Aurora 7, Aurora 7,*" astronaut Gus Grissom repeated urgently into the microphone before him at Mercury Control Center. "Do you read me? Do you read me?" Grissom was trying to make radio contact with fellow astronaut Scott Carpenter aboard the Mercury space capsule *Aurora 7*. The date was May 24, 1962, and Carpenter had just completed three loops around Earth, becoming the second American to fly in orbit. Now, moments after the scheduled time for splashdown, his capsule was supposed to be riding the Atlantic swell, with Carpenter safe and dry inside. But why didn't he answer?

The quiet monotone of Grissom's voice was the loudest sound in the room at Cape Canaveral, Florida. He and everyone else in Mercury Control knew that Carpenter's flight had not gone entirely according to plan.

The trouble had started as Carpenter, hurtling along at five miles per second, began his return to Earth. The first step in this stage of the mission was to fire the capsule's thrusters — small, rocket-like nozzles that controlled the spacecraft's orientation during flight — and thereby tilt *Aurora 7* to the proper angle for return to Earth. The next step was to apply the capsule's brakes, called retrorockets, in order to slow the craft, sending it earthward. When *Aurora 7* had descended to an altitude of about 25,000 feet, parachutes were to pop open and lower the capsule gently onto the sea.

But one thing after another went wrong. When Carpenter was called upon to position *Aurora 7* for return to Earth, the capsule's automatic stabilization system for some reason was unable to hold the spacecraft at the correct angle for re-entering the atmosphere. Carpenter responded by switching to manual control, but he inadvertently misaligned the capsule by 25 degrees. To make matters worse, the retrorockets fired three seconds late and, because of the capsule's misalignment, they delivered less braking power than expected.

Entering Earth's atmosphere in a spacecraft pitched at the wrong angle and traveling too fast can turn a craft and its astronaut to cinders. Happily, in this instance the combined effect of the errors merely hurled Carpenter some 250 miles beyond the intended point of splashdown — and well beyond the range both of Gus Grissom's voice radio and of the naval force, led by an aircraft carrier, that had been assigned to recover *Aurora 7*. For nine minutes after reentry, Gus Grissom and the others at the Cape did not know for certain whether Carpenter was dead or alive, much less where he might be.

DIGITAL GUARDIANS POINT THE WAY

But a pair of machines knew almost exactly where Carpenter was. Hundreds of miles away at the Goddard Space Flight Center in Maryland, two mainframe computers had monitored his errant return to Earth. After Carpenter fired *Aurora 7's* retrorockets, these machines digested position and altitude data supplied by a radar ground station in California that tracked *Aurora 7* as it sped overhead toward the Atlantic. Then, 11 minutes after the capsule's last radio contact with the California tracking station, one of the computers issued a remarkably accurate estimate of the capsule's whereabouts. According to the machine's calculations, the spacecraft would be found floating approximately 125 miles northeast of Puerto Rico.

Aircraft dispatched by the recovery task force rushed toward the scene and quickly homed in on the signal from *Aurora 7's* radio beacon, which Carpenter had turned on at splashdown. Just over half an hour after the capsule hit the water, a crewman on one of the search planes spotted the astronaut riding an inflatable life raft alongside his spacecraft, which bobbed in the water like an inverted funnel. Some two and a half hours later, Carpenter was hoisted safely aboard a Navy helicopter.

At the time of *Aurora 7's* flight, not everyone in the space business had accepted computers as necessary partners. Aerospace engineers, astronauts and ground controllers tended to regard the machines with wariness. As in other applications, computers employed for space flight sometimes ceased to function for no apparent reason. The programs instructing them were already among the most intricate that software experts had yet been called upon to write, and the slightest error could result in disaster. Moreover, the complexity of computer programs for space flight could mask a fatal mistake in the code that might surface only when preceded by the most unlikely concatenation of events — and when the hour for correcting the error might be long past.

Yet exploration of space could not proceed far without them. The planets in their orbits wait for no man to calculate, err and then recalculate how much rocket thrust is necessary, applied at what instant and for how long in order to journey from one point in the heavens to another and return in safety. Only computers could absorb the flood of data produced by devices as complicated as spacecraft in circumstances as alien as space flight — and then weigh the information and help humans render correct and timely decisions.

During five decades of practical rocketry, computers have indeed proved themselves indispensable to every phase of space flight. They assist in the design of space vehicles and check to ensure that they are in good working order before flight. Computers simulate missions in space so that engineers can test the behavior of spacecraft and rocket boosters in the laboratory, and so that astronauts can hone their skills on practice flights without ever leaving terra firma. Computers also choreograph the thousands of details leading to the launch of a spacecraft and, once the mission is under way, monitor its progress from the ground. Increasingly, computers have been pressed into service aboard spacecraft heading deep into the void, beyond the range of instantaneous communications with Earth: Unmanned voyages to the farthest planets of the solar system are almost entirely under the control of rugged, on-board computers, programmed in advance with instructions and contingency plans for their encounters with heavenly bodies.

THE PIONEERS

Looking back, the ubiquity of computers in space exploration seems inevitable, but it was not always clear how or even if they could make a contribution. The application of computers to space flight dates to the early days of World War II, when a team of German engineers began experiments combining computers with rocketry at a research center near the village of Peenemünde, on a remote island off Germany's Baltic coast. One day, members of the group would help Americans fly to the moon; and at the time, under the direction of a brilliant and hard-driving civilian named Wernher von Braun, the team was already experimenting at the edge of space, launching liquid-fueled rockets into the upper reaches of Earth's atmosphere.

Von Braun belonged to a generation that, in the early decades of the 20th century, saw the possibility of realizing humankind's age-old dream of space travel. A new technology was emerging. Throughout Europe, in the United States and in the Soviet Union, groups of rocketry enthusiasts launched missile after missile in their attempts to build rockets powerful enough to overcome Earth's gravity and blast into space. In many countries, these pioneers gained reputations as impractical fanatics. However, in Germany they were taken very seriously, especially by the armed forces. At the end of World War I, the German military had been prohibited by the Treaty of Versailles from developing specific kinds of armaments, heavy artillery among them. But the treaty was full of loopholes. Though artillery was proscribed, there was no mention of rockets. Thus, the German army was free to investigate them as an alternative to cannons. It did so eagerly, first by funding experiments von Braun performed at Kummersdorf, a research center near Berlin, and later, in 1935, by starting up the research center at Peenemünde.

Most of the engineers who worked under von Braun at Peenemünde were fervent advocates of space travel, as he was: Hitler's Gestapo once arrested von Braun on the charge, among other accusations, that he was more interested in space research than in developing rockets for warfare. Yet the team's principal achievement — a rocket named the Assembly-4, or A-4 for short — could stand as good evidence to the contrary. With a range of nearly 200 miles and a warhead containing more than a ton of high explosives, the A-4 was a formidable tool of destruction. Renamed by the Nazi propaganda ministry after the German word for "vengeance weapon," it began to savage London in September 1944 as the fearsome V-2.

Inside the V-2 was a small computer that helped guide the missile to its distant targets. The device was invented by a young electrical engineer named Helmut Hoelzer, who came up with the basic concept in 1935 while still a student at the Technical University of Darmstadt. Like many other students, he spent much of his spare time piloting gliders, a fad that arose from the same circumstances that had fostered German rocket science. "According to the Treaty of Versailles," Hoelzer explained years later, "there was not much Germany was allowed to do in aviation." So, recounted Hoelzer, the Germans said, " 'Okay, if we cannot use motors, then we do it without motors,' and so motorless flight became a very popular sport among the young people at that time."

Hoelzer found one feature of the sport an irritation. Although the aircraft's instrument panel had a prominent gauge that showed how fast the glider was slicing through the air, it lacked a device for measuring speed relative to the ground. (The two speeds would be equal only on a windless day.) Resolving to design a gadget that would tell him how fast the terrain was slipping by below him, Hoelzer remembered studying a mechanical computing device designed by Vannevar Bush at the Massachusetts Institute of Technology in 1927.

An elephantine assemblage of shafts and gears that ran the length of a big room, it was known as a differential analyzer. Its purpose was to solve differential equations, complex mathematical expressions used to predict the behavior of moving objects such as airplanes.

The analyzer operated far too slowly for use in calculating the speed of a glider. So Hoelzer hit upon the notion of replacing Bush's gears and shafts with an electronic apparatus — a computer, in effect — that would solve differential equations fast enough to serve as a speedometer and that would be compact enough to fit inside an aircraft. His idea was to set up an arrangement of weights and springs that could sense acceleration in much the same way that a passenger in an automobile feels pressed against the seat as a car speeds up. In essence, his invention would translate that force into an electric current that could be measured and used to calculate the aircraft's speed almost instantaneously. Like Bush's differential analyzer, this would be an analog computer. In contrast to digital computers, which manipulate information in digital, on-off form, analog devices represent data with physical variables such as the movement of gears or variations in the magnitude of an electrical voltage.

Hoelzer proposed that he build the speedometer as part of his undergraduate

10

work. Unfortunately, the head of his department deemed the project too expensive and ambitious, and he turned it down. But Hoelzer resurrected the idea in 1939, two years after earning his master's degree, when he was ordered to Peenemünde by the Nazi government.

At that time, the V-2 had a rudimentary gyroscopic system capable of controlling the missile in the three axes of flight: pitch and yaw — rotations about two axes at right angles to each other and to the length of the rocket — and roll, or rotation about the lengthwise axis of the missile (page 52). Such control was essential to prevent the thrust of the rocket engine at one end of the missile from flipping it end over end. However, the system was imperfect. One problem lay in some of the gyroscopes. Called rate gyros, they measured how fast the missile turned about each axis of rotation so that such motions could be damped; the rate gyros were so sensitive to the shock and vibration of launch that they were all too likely to fail. But even if the rate gyros had been reliable, the rocket might still miss its target by a wide margin because of a second imperfection: The system was unable to detect or correct for the missile being blown sideways by the wind.

When Hoelzer arrived at Peenemünde, he went to work with the group responsible for improving the V-2's control system. He was to help turn it into a true guidance system with the addition of drift correction. The guidance-system team was approaching the drift problem from two directions. The first was to thwart drift by means of a radio beam transmitted from a ground installation situated a half dozen or so miles behind the launch pad. The transmission was such that a specially designed radio receiver aboard the rocket could detect whether the missile had strayed from the beam's center. The second drift-sensing approach was to use accelerometers, each an arrangement of springs and weights similar to that planned by Hoelzer for his glider speedometer.

The radio-beam tactic, because it extended practices already proven in radio-controlled aircraft, was further along than the accelerometer solution, which depended first on the perfection of a rugged yet sensitive assembly of weights and springs. But radio signals — and therefore the accuracy of the V-2 — were subject to disruption by the Allies, a weakness not shared by an inertial guidance system based on accelerometers. So work proceeded intensely on both fronts.

FROM GLIDERS TO ROCKETS

Hoelzer saw immediately that his plan for a glider speedometer could be applied with a few modifications to correct sideways drift in the V-2. After all, the question was the same for both vehicles: How fast was it traveling relative to the ground? He began by working out ways of representing mathematical functions — addition, subtraction, multiplication, division and other, more complicated concepts — as circuits made of capacitors, resistors and other electronic components. By combining such circuits appropriately, Hoelzer assembled an electronic computer that could represent complex equations of motion. Supplied with an electric current generated by the guidance system as winds blew the rocket off course, the computer could calculate the sideways speed of the missile. Graphite steering vanes in the exhaust stream would then be activated to correct the rocket's course.

If Hoelzer's computer could calculate the velocity of drift, a linear motion, only minor redesign was required for it to handle the circular motions of pitch, roll or yaw around the three axes of flight. Hoelzer revised the device to accomplish just that, and soon it supplanted the over-sensitive rate gyros with electronic circuits so sturdy that they rarely failed. Furthermore, each of these electronic "gyros" cost only about $2.50; the rate gyros they replaced cost $7,000 each.

Hoelzer's success with his electronic guidance and control computer inspired him to adapt the idea for another purpose. Test flights to examine V-2 guidance-system performance were seldom informative; the missile typically crashed at sea and exploded or sank, leaving no trace of what went wrong or right. Peenemünde engineers had taken steps toward a solution by suspending a V-2 above the ground and shoving it from side to side with a system of heavy weights and springs to simulate a V-2's motions. But this approach was time-consuming and expensive, and it could not imitate some of the forces that affected a V-2 after launch. Hoelzer's plan was to build an analog computer that would mimic the rocket's behavior in flight and test its guidance system.

A COOL RECEPTION

Not all of Hoelzer's colleagues shared his enthusiasm for computers. One superior, mathematician Hermann Steuding, held little hope for the success of Hoelzer's simulation work — "machines cannot do this" — and had a low opinion of computers in general. "Young man," Steuding once said to Hoelzer, "when I compute something, the results will be correct and I do not need a machine to verify it." Even Wernher von Braun saw little promise in Hoelzer's work and advised him to "quit playing with electronic toys."

But Hoelzer persisted in secret. Time being of the essence in war-ravaged Germany, he enlisted a fellow engineer, Otto Hirschler, to help. The two men began building a rough model of the device in a small room that could be reached only through Hoelzer's office. They finished their backroom prototype in 1941 and demonstrated it for von Braun and the other top brass, who enthusiastically ordered the two engineers to build an operational version. The completed apparatus, which stood about five feet high and was powered in part by a vacuum-cleaner motor, soon went into regular service, testing new guidance systems before they were installed in missiles.

Hoelzer prepared a doctoral dissertation based on the design of the machine and submitted the paper to the Technical University at Darmstadt in late 1945, soon after the war ended. By then, the university was under the control of a U.S. Army captain, a member of the military government overseeing occupied Germany. Hoelzer later recalled that the captain rejected the dissertation because it involved "weapons development" and because "rockets are not necessary anymore" since there would be no more war. When Hoelzer pointed out that rockets could also be used for space flight, the captain brushed aside such notions as "fantasies."

On the advice of one of his prewar professors, Hoelzer revised the dissertation by splitting it in two. In the first part, which was to be presented to the captain, he removed all references to rockets. The second part, which described the application of his analog computers to rocketry, was intended only for the eyes of the German faculty. As a result of this Solomonic ploy, Hoelzer in February 1946 received the first doctorate ever awarded for research in computer science.

Shortly thereafter, Hoelzer emigrated to the United States. He eventually went to work at the U.S. Army's Redstone Arsenal in Huntsville, Alabama, joining von Braun and more than 100 other members of the Peenemünde team, whom the army had recruited at the end of the war. Along with sufficient V-2 components to assemble about 100 missiles, the Germans had brought with them one of Hoelzer's analog computers. The missiles became the foundation for postwar rocket development in America, and Hoelzer's invention proved invaluable, as did other analog devices that the computer spawned.

The group's first major accomplishment for the army was the Redstone missile. Essentially an improved V-2 with a range of 200 miles, it was guided by an analog computer invented by James Farrior, a young American who had joined the team. This computer was an improvement on Hoelzer's designs in that it controlled range as well as drift. Farrior's device was the forerunner of many similar guidance computers.

In 1956, the Huntsville group stacked two clusters of smaller, solid-propellant rockets, one inside the other, atop the Redstone to make a new rocket called the Jupiter C. The first of Jupiter C's two upper stages, as they were known, was to be ignited after the first-stage Redstone had consumed its fuel and had been separated from the upper stages to fall earthward. When the second stage was spent, it would drop away so that the third stage could be fired. These stepwise reductions in the weight of the rocket as its fuel was consumed would make it possible for rocket engines of modest power to launch packages of scientific instruments into orbit.

But before the Jupiter C could demonstrate its prowess, it was spectacularly upstaged. On October 4, 1957, the Soviet Union launched the first man-made satellite, the 184-pound *Sputnik I*. The feat dealt a severe jolt to the United States' confidence in its position as world leader in technology. Not only were the Russians first, but *Sputnik I* weighed almost six times as much as the satellite that the Americans were working on. And if *Sputnik I* were not sobering enough, Russian space scientists a month later sent *Sputnik II* into orbit, carrying the world's first space traveler, a dog named Laika. In response to the Soviet accomplishments and the climate of cold-war competition, America shifted its space program into high gear and began to expand it at a pace that von Braun and his space-travel enthusiasts once had only dreamed of.

After three months of fevered preparation, a modified Jupiter C took off on January 31, 1958, propelling *Explorer I,* a 31-pound package that included 18 pounds of scientific instruments, into orbit to become America's first artificial satellite. It was followed two months later by a three-and-one-quarter-pound satellite sent aloft aboard *Vanguard I,* a rocket that was developed by the U.S. Naval Research Laboratory. In July 1958, the National Aeronautics and Space Administration (NASA) was created. Three months later, the new agency authorized Project Mercury, the United States' effort to place an astronaut in orbit.

Over the next two years, preparations for the Mercury project advanced amid intense publicity and mounting national excitement. Then the Russians outshone the U.S. again. On April 12, 1961, the Soviet Union launched the first manned space mission, a single orbit of Earth by cosmonaut Yuri Gagarin. Six weeks later, President John F. Kennedy went before Congress and, rising dramatically to the latest Russian challenge, announced that the United States would commit its resources to landing a man on the moon "before this decade is out."

Meeting the goals of Project Mercury and the moon program required a massive push on technological fronts, especially that of computers. The analog devices pioneered at Peenemünde continued to play an important role in the simulation of rocket flight and in keeping the rockets on course after launch. But as the manned space program progressed, the big electronic digital computers that had emerged from wartime research in the U.S. assumed a leading role.

In the beginning, few people in the new space agency could predict exactly what part computers would play in the space program. "Hell, in those days, nobody on my project knew anything about either computers or space," recalled Bill Tindall, a mechanical engineer who in 1948, at the age of 23, had gone to work for NASA's predecessor, the National Advisory Committee for Aeronautics (NACA). One of Tindall's jobs at NACA, before the agency was absorbed into NASA, was working on Project Echo, an inflatable communications satellite scheduled to be launched in 1960. The composition of the gases inside the balloon required that Echo stay constantly in the sunlight to ensure that it remained inflated. To keep Echo warm, precise and complex calculations were needed to determine the time of launch and the trajectory of the rocket that would send it into orbit.

To work out those computations, Tindall and a colleague, Eugene Davis, turned to NACA's IBM 650 computer. Neither man had any experience with computers or programming. "So Gene got a book," said Tindall, "and taught

Milestones of Spaceborne Computing

The role of computers in the space program has been an evolutionary one, beginning with analog devices, used to guide early rockets, and simple sequencers aboard the first unmanned probes. The time line that starts at right and continues on the following pages lists some of the significant computers, components and automated systems that are featured in this book. Manned flight computer milestones are marked by black dots; open dots indicate unmanned space projects. Dates generally refer to operational debuts — that is, the year a system or component was first employed on a mission. Computer languages and automated check-out systems, which were phased into use gradually and modified over time, are dated according to the year the initial design was introduced.

○ V-2 guidance and control computer: analog device used to control German V-2 rocket.

○ V-2 simulator: analog computer adapted for rocket flight simulation (used to test V-2).

1941

himself and me orbital mechanics and then how to write programs for orbital trajectories.'' Tindall's newfound knowledge earned him a reputation as a computer expert at NASA. He was put in charge of software development for the computer system that would serve as the nerve center for a worldwide communications and radar-tracking network established to monitor and control the 26 missions planned for the Mercury project.

Built at a cost of $100 million, the network comprised a score of ground and ship-based stations spanning three oceans and three continents. These stations, linked by approximately 177,000 miles of telephone, teletype and computer communications wire, were designed to establish a radio link for conversations with the astronaut when the spacecraft was in range. The stations would also receive from the spacecraft radio signals known as telemetry, which provided a stream of information about such vitals as the astronaut's heart rate and body temperature, as well as the amount of fuel remaining for the capsule's automatic attitude-control system.

Radar at each station would track the spacecraft, providing position reports that would enable computers to calculate the capsule's velocity and predict its course. With this information, each successive tracking station could position its antennas to communicate with the capsule the moment it came over the horizon. And in the event of an emergency, the computers could tell mission controllers when it was safe to interrupt a flight so that the capsule would descend to a water landing.

The tracking network was set up by the Western Electric Company, which

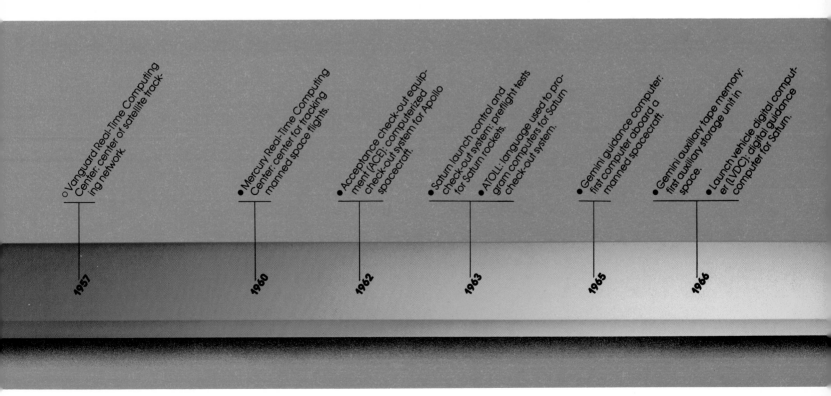

o Vanguard Real-Time Computing Center: center of satellite tracking network.

1957

Mercury Real-Time Computing Center: center for tracking manned space flights.

1960

Acceptance check-out equipment (ACE); computerized check-out system for Apollo spacecraft.

1962

Saturn launch control and check-out system; preflight tests for Saturn rockets.

ATOLL: language used to program computers for Saturn check-out system.

1963

Gemini guidance computer: first computer aboard a manned spacecraft.

1965

Gemini auxiliary tape memory: first auxiliary storage unit in space.

Launch vehicle digital computer (LVDC): digital guidance computer for Saturn.

1966

engaged IBM to provide the necessary computers and software. In 1957, IBM had supplied one of its machines — the 709 model, packed with old-fashioned vacuum tubes — to help track the Project Vanguard satellite. The computer, installed in Washington, D.C., ran a 40,000-instruction program that provided trajectory calculations in real time. Generally speaking, the concept of real time performance means that a computer operates rapidly enough to solve problems and handle events as they occur. For orbital missions, manned or unmanned, real time meant fast enough so that tracking stations could establish contact with a satellite as soon as it came over the horizon.

IBM chose its newer 7090 model mainframe for Project Mercury. The 7090 had been developed to satisfy Department of Defense requirements for the new Ballistic Missile Early Warning System (BMEWS), intended to alert the United States to a possible attack by intercontinental ballistic missiles. During such an attack, BMEWS and its computers, like the Mercury stations, would be required to track rapidly moving objects across the heavens. In this computer, transistors replaced the bulky vacuum tubes of the earlier model.

The IBM 7090 suited NASA perfectly. Not only had it demonstrated competence in a similar role, but NASA's machines were essentially identical to those that IBM sold commercially, an important consideration. From NASA's inception, the agency had been intensely concerned with the safety of its astronauts. This led to a policy that dictated the use of proven equipment and technology wherever possible, and the 7090 filled the bill.

The quest for safety also necessitated the installation of not one but two 7090s,

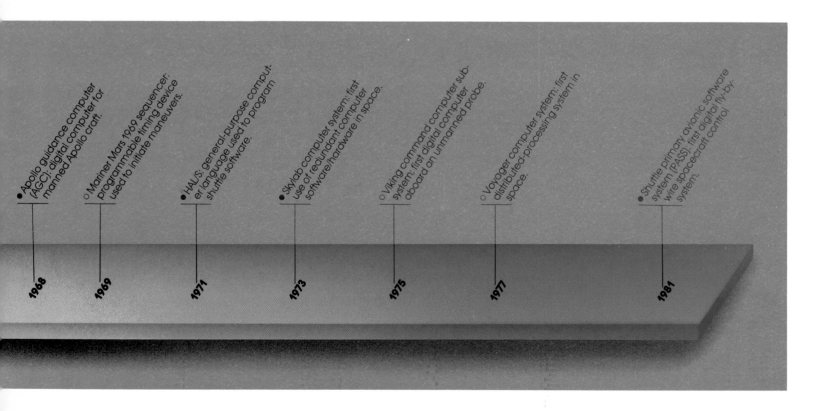

the second machine serving as a "hot backup," in space agency jargon. The 7090s would operate in parallel, with each receiving the same information as the other. Only one machine—designated the prime computer, or mission operational computer—was permitted to transmit its output. But the other machine, dubbed the dynamic stand-by, could swing into action at the flip of a switch if something were to go awry with the prime computer.

NASA decided to install the computers at the new Goddard Space Flight Center, then under construction in Maryland, less than 30 minutes from downtown Washington, D.C. From there, they would be in contact via special telephone lines with another pair of machines at Cape Canaveral, the Air Force missile test range chosen as the launch site for the Mercury missions. One of the Cape computers, a Burroughs machine connected to radar, was delegated to guide the rocket after lift-off. The second computer at Mercury Control Center, an IBM 709, analyzed radar data about the booster's position for the range safety officer, who was responsible for destroying wayward rockets that posed a threat to those below.

The 800-mile distance between Goddard and the Cape dictated one important modification that distinguished Mercury's 7090s from the commercial variety. IBM engineers developed for the project a special device called an IBM 7281 Data Communications Channel, which permitted four channels of communication between the 7090 prime computer and the Cape instead of the usual two; one pair for input and another for output.

Data moved between Goddard and the Cape on a special leased telephone line that could transmit 1,000 bits per second. At the time, that rate was considered extraordinarily rapid; 25 years later, even inexpensive home microcomputers could transmit information faster, routinely sending 1,200 bits per second over ordinary telephone wires.

NASA's policy of redundancy—having a backup ready to take over in the event of failure—called for the data lines of the input and output pairs to be routed separately. However, many months later it came to light that the telephone company had bundled all the lines together in a single cable running from Goddard to the local phone office. "We discovered this one day when all four went out," recalled Bill Tindall. A blast from "a hunter's shotgun ruptured the cable," he explained. "Needless to say, the idea of redundancy was in the right place, but the cables weren't." Fortunately, the incident occurred between missions, and the lines could be repaired and rerouted before the next flight.

ROUGHING IT IN THE SPACE AGE
The Goddard center was still unfinished in late 1960 when the two 7090s moved in. The raw concrete shell of the building that housed them had temporary plywood walls and a canvas roof. Inside, plywood partitions divided the space, except for the computer room. It was complete and equipped with portable air conditioners to cool the computers. But there were no handrails in the stair wells, and a trip to the bathroom meant a hike through the woods to a finished building. Dust, a threat to any computer's sensitive innards, was a nagging problem. "We were cleaning all the time," said Tindall, whose software group arrived at Goddard along with the machines.

The team, which included programmers from IBM, faced a formidable challenge in developing software to meet the Mercury network's requirements. At the time, a computer had to finish running one program before another could begin; once a series of mathematical calculations was initiated, for example, it could not be interrupted until it was completed. Furthermore, the central processing unit, which performed the calculations, could not operate while the computer was receiving or sending data, or while peripheral devices such as printers were working. But Goddard Space Flight Center needed its computers to perform three jobs concurrently: to receive data from Cape Canaveral and the tracking stations, to process the information and then to send out the results soon enough for them to be useful.

To permit the system to handle a number of jobs at once, the IBM experts developed a special control program called the Mercury Monitor. A precursor of what today is known as an operating system, the Mercury Monitor functioned as a kind of electronic traffic cop. It organized the transmission of data so that the computer's central processing unit did not have to give the process its undivided attention. The Monitor also provided a mechanism to suspend a program when another program of higher priority had to operate. Electronic markers identifying such priorities — for example, that processing data from the Mercury Control Center at Cape Canaveral took precedence over printing a table of figures — were built into the programs. Recognizing priorities among programs was quite a feat for a computer in 1960 — and an accomplishment that Tindall and the IBM team were understandably proud of.

PRACTICE MAKES PERFECT
In the months before the pair of 7090s with their Mercury Monitor were called upon to serve a real mission, they took part in countless dress rehearsals. Special programs mimicked all three phases of a flight — launch, orbit and reentry — by generating make-believe trajectory and telemetry data to put the computers through their paces. Mercury Control Center and the remote tracking stations were also bombarded with phony malfunctions to see if they could cope with problems that might arise on a real mission. In trial after trial, the system performed flawlessly.

But the real test came on February 20, 1962. That morning at 6:03, as the overcast sky began to clear over Cape Canaveral, Marine lieutenant colonel John Glenn, a 40-year-old Ohioan, eased himself feetfirst into the spacecraft designated *Friendship 7*. Weighing two tons, the Mercury capsule perched atop a booster rocket that was adapted especially for the Mercury program — the Atlas. It towered 10 stories above the launch pad, and when fired up, it would produce four times the thrust of the modified Jupiter C that had launched *Explorer I*.

The year before, only months after Yuri Gagarin's orbital flight, two of Glenn's comrades, Mercury astronauts Alan Shepard and Gus Grissom, had each been rocketed by Wernher von Braun's Redstone boosters to an altitude of about 115 miles, arching high over the atmosphere in a ballistic curve and then splashing down in the Atlantic. John Glenn was the astronaut chosen for America's first manned orbital flight.

As technicians strapped Glenn into the custom-molded seat of his capsule, the computer crew at Goddard Space Flight Center was running last-minute checks on the tracking network and the communications links between the computers in Maryland and those at the Cape. Everything had been going smoothly when, 90 minutes before the scheduled lift-off, lights on the computer console blinked out. The prime computer had ceased to function.

Computer section head John Morton, who later described himself as already "scared to death" by the prospect of the system's debut, was well rehearsed for such a crisis. Instantly, he ordered one of the two computer operators hovering over the machines to switch to the dynamic stand-by computer, which assumed its new responsibilities without a stumble. Within minutes, technicians had resuscitated the prime computer, which uneventfully assumed its former role. (The problem was so minor that, 25 years later, Morton could not remember exactly what it was.)

Thanks to having a spare machine ready to go, not a moment was lost in the countdown. At 9:47 a.m., flames burst from the exhaust nozzles of the Atlas engines, initiating Glenn's historic journey and an intricately orchestrated performance by the quartet of mission-control computers.

The Burroughs machine at the Cape was already receiving a stream of radio signals from sensors connected to the booster's guidance system. Thirty seconds after lift-off, the computer began using this data to calculate the rocket's position, speed and direction of flight. Then it generated commands, transmitted by radio to the guidance system, that steered the booster along the proper trajectory toward the point where — if all went according to plan — the spacecraft would separate from the top of the Atlas and go into orbit.

Meanwhile, the IBM 709 range-safety computer was also tracking the booster by means of radar based at Cape Canaveral. As it received the data, the 709 issued a series of reports confirming for the range-safety officer that the rocket was on course. A third radar, located in Bermuda along with yet another IBM 709 computer, began tracking the rocket as soon as it came into view, providing a third estimate of altitude, trajectory and speed.

Data from all three computers was transmitted simultaneously to Goddard, where the 7090s analyzed the information to help controllers make the critical decision as to whether the launch was Go or No Go for orbit. The computers were to determine whether the spacecraft had attained sufficient speed and altitude to circle Earth at least once. If so, a Go signal would be passed to the Cape and immediately thereafter to *Friendship 7*. If not, the Space Flight Center would send countdown instructions for Glenn to fire the capsule's retro-rockets in time for a safe landing in the recovery area already designated for such an emergency.

Time was of the essence. After the engines of the Atlas had cut off and explosive bolts had automatically detonated to separate the capsule from the booster, the Goddard computer would have no more than 10 seconds to render its advice. A delay in the event of a No Go could doom the capsule to a crash landing in Africa.

At 9:52 a.m., five minutes after launch, John Glenn got a Go. His *Friendship 7* had reached a speed of more than 17,500 miles per hour, slipping smoothly into orbit.

As Glenn began his journey eastward, the computers at Goddard settled into their routines. From each remote station in turn came radar information on *Friendship 7's* position. The primary computer poured out a constant stream of information about the capsule's location, speed and predicted path. Relayed to the tracking stations, this information enabled them to promptly lock onto the spacecraft with radio and radar as it came into range. At the same time, the information went to Mercury Control at Cape Canaveral, where *Friendship 7's* progress around the globe was plotted on a large, flattened map of the globe.

Less than five hours after he had left Earth, as Glenn neared completion of his third orbit, the Goddard computers undertook their final task, calculating the precise instant for the astronaut to fire the retrorockets in order to bring the capsule down in its Atlantic recovery area. As it happened, *Friendship 7* splashed down some 40 miles short of the predicted point of impact. Humans forgot to instruct the computer to take into account a lessening of the spacecraft's weight caused by the use of consumables such as oxygen, water and a snack of applesauce, which the astronaut's body converted to heat during the flight.

Though the error did not slow the recovery of Glenn and his spacecraft — a ship pulled alongside the capsule 17 minutes after splashdown — the program was quickly corrected. Computers and programs were thus in proper form to predict accurately the 250-mile overshoot when Scott Carpenter became the second American to return from orbit three months later.

In all, there were six manned Mercury missions. The final one, the flight of *Faith 7*, took place on May 15, 1963. Piloted by astronaut Gordon Cooper, *Faith 7* circled Earth 22 times. Throughout the Mercury program, the ground-control computer system functioned splendidly. Occasional tweaking of the software improved performance in minor ways, but the system remained fundamentally unchanged during those exciting early months of the United States' manned space-flight program. All was in order for the next step in the adventure of traveling to the moon — Project Gemini.

Digital Exercises in Illusion

Manned space flight is risky business. Complicated equipment (the space shuttle and its rocket engines have thousands of moving parts) endures tremendous strain at launch and afterward is exposed to radiation and temperatures more intense than anything encountered on Earth.

The great probability is that sometime during a flight something will go wrong. The failure could well be catastrophic, like the leaking booster that caused the space shuttle *Challenger* to explode in 1986. More than likely, however, the problem will be a smaller one that need not doom a mission if the crew knows what to do about it and acts in time.

To prepare for uneventful missions as well as ones in which major difficulties arise, NASA has long used machines to simulate space flight. Simulators train both the astronauts who venture into space and the flight controllers who remain on the ground. Though expensive to build and operate, these technological marvels make manned space flight practical. Without them, it is doubtful whether any nation would accept the risks of sending astronauts into space.

As spacecraft have grown more complex, so have the machines and computers that mimic their exploits. The space-shuttle simulator *(overleaf)* is so complicated that rank upon rank of computers are necessary in order to emulate the spacecraft's flight systems, to let astronauts work the manipulator arm in the payload bay — which appears in one simulator only as computer-generated graphics — and to present astronauts in training with some of the multitude of problems that might arise on a real mission. The result is a computer system substantially more powerful than the five IBM machines that ride the actual shuttle into space. And the experiences the computers produce are so grueling that even veteran astronauts leave the simulator sweating and exhausted.

Half an Acre of Computerized Magic

Open for business 16 hours a day, five days a week, the Shuttle Mission Simulator Facility *(below)* occupies 21,500 square feet of floor space at the Johnson Space Center in Houston, Texas. Inside are three master conjurors — computerized simulators so convincing in their illusions that astronauts who practice in them for future shuttle missions readily accept the fraud.

The simulators duplicate parts of the space shuttle's cabin layout. One simulator, called the motion-base crew station, matches the tilts, turns and vibrations of the shuttle during launch and landing and, along with the fixed-base crew sta-tion, trains astronauts for tasks to be performed in orbit, such as the satellite launch recounted on the following pages. A third, the Spacelab simulator, familiarizes crew members with the Spacelab, a module that fits inside the shuttle's payload bay and carries scientific experiments into space.

Taken together, the three crew stations occupy only about one sixth of the simulator facility. The rest of the area is packed with computers and supporting equipment. All told, there are more than 30 computers divided among the three simulators. For example, to operate the fixed-base crew station, a large host computer generates flight-deck sound effects and coordinates 17 other computers. A dozen of them supply instrument-panel displays, provide a representation of the manipulator arm used for work in the payload bay and generate views of Earth and the stars in space as they would appear during an actual mission. The other five perform the activities of the computers aboard a real shuttle.

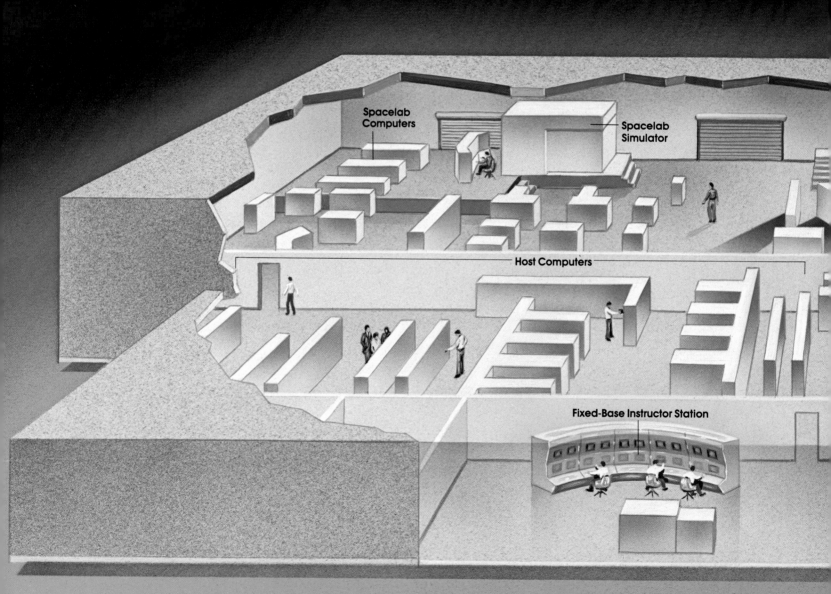

Spacelab Computers

Spacelab Simulator

Host Computers

Fixed-Base Instructor Station

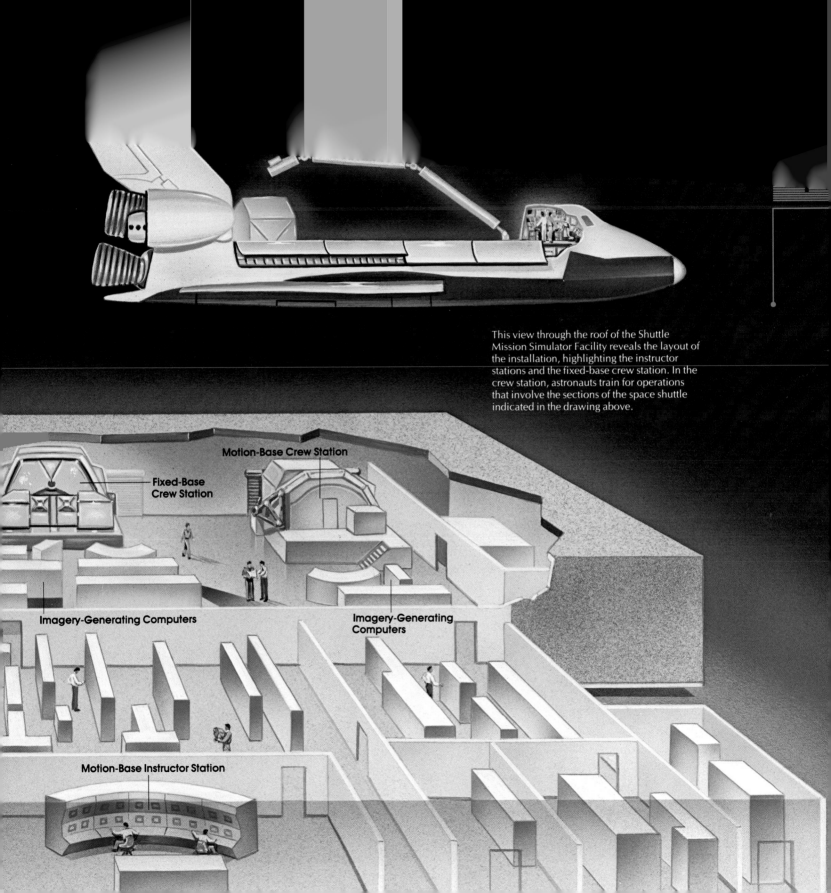

This view through the roof of the Shuttle Mission Simulator Facility reveals the layout of the installation, highlighting the instructor stations and the fixed-base crew station. In the crew station, astronauts train for operations that involve the sections of the space shuttle indicated in the drawing above.

Motion-Base Crew Station

Fixed-Base Crew Station

Imagery-Generating Computers

Imagery-Generating Computers

Motion-Base Instructor Station

Prelude to a Space-Shuttle Simulation

In the crew space of the fixed-base crew station (left), astronauts training for a flight prepare to practice the mission's premier objective — to launch a satellite from the shuttle's payload bay into Earth orbit. In some training sessions, the simulation begins with the shuttle launch from Cape Canaveral; but on this occasion, the focus is sharper. As the simulation gets under way, the shuttle has recently arrived in orbit: The objective for today is to release the satellite on schedule.

While instructors sitting at their consoles ready the simulator, the four crew members make final preparations for the exercise. The astronaut seated near the center of the illustration will perform the role of mission commander, and the pilot, sitting to his right, will act as his assistant. The two mission specialists behind them will deploy the satellite.

Whenever an astronaut moves a control, pushes a button or flips a switch inside the simulator, computers react instantly to mimic the real-world results of such actions (below). Depending on the situation, cockpit displays flash new information to the crew; instrument-panel lights turn on or off; new views appear in the windows; and realistic sounds of motors whirring, fans blowing and thrusters hissing emanate from hidden speakers.

The Computers behind the Scene

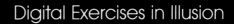

Host Computer

On-Board Computers

Imagery-Generating Computers

Simulation-Management Computer

Crew-Station Computer

To the simulator's computers, a switch thrown or a lever pulled is a request for information about the shuttle's response to the stimulus. The request travels through the crew-station computer, which handles the flow of data to and from the instrument and control panels, to the simulation-management computer, where data from the crew, instructor and operator stations converge. This machine passes the request to the simulator's on-board computers, which in a real flight receive signals directly from the control panel on the flight deck. The on-board computers issue commands for the shuttle to respond to the crew's actions. These orders are intercepted by the host computer. After calculating the simulator's reaction, the host sends the results in three directions: to on-board computers to indicate that a response has occurred; to management and crew-station computers to update instrument-panel displays for the crew; and to imagery-generating computers, which determine what to show through the windows and the lenses of simulated TV cameras in the payload bay and on the manipulator arm.

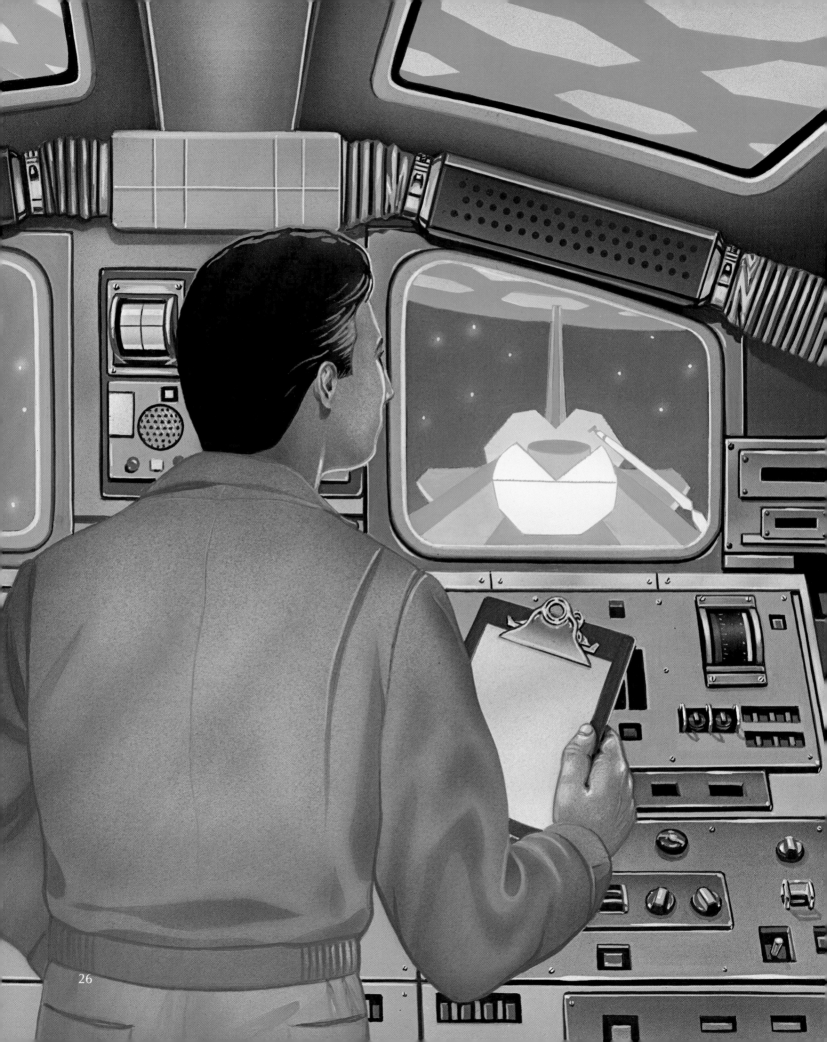

Cruising Along in Earth Orbit

Having reached simulated orbit, the mission specialist activates the shuttle's payload-bay doors, which disappear from view when fully opened to reveal the satellite inside a protective sun shield. Upon completing a cursory visual inspection and reading its vital signs from a display on the flight deck, the mission specialist will close the sun shield by remote control.

Everything that the astronauts see of the world outside the crew space — payload-bay doors opening, the satellite in the sun shield, a crudely represented Earth floating overhead — is provided by means of an elaborate projection system. Computers select components from a collection of 50,000 images. They assemble these pieces into scenes at the rate of 25 frames each second in order to impart a realistic flow to motion. Then the images are projected into the windows *(below)*.

Through a Window Electronically

A projection system surrounds the fixed-base crew station to cast computer-generated images of the world outside the shuttle against one or more mirrors and into the shuttle's windows. En route, the images pass through optical refractors, which provide an illusion of depth and of changing perspective as crew members move about the cabin.

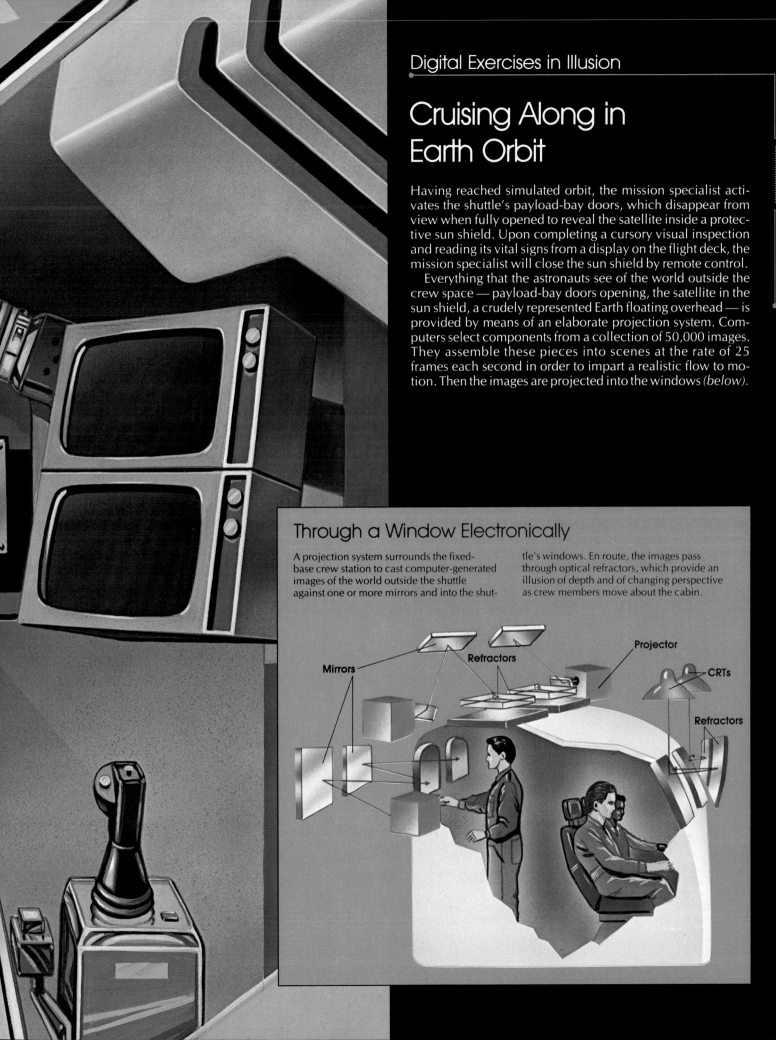

Mirrors

Refractors

Projector

CRTs

Refractors

A Spanner
in the Works

A few hours into this flight, the time approaches to deploy the satellite. As on a real mission, there is a launch window of only 15 minutes. If the satellite release occurs before the window opens or after it closes, a multimillion-dollar investment will be positioned in an orbit where it might be useless.

Well ahead of time, the mission commander rolls the spacecraft so that the payload-bay opening, which points earthward for much of the mission to help regulate the shuttle's temperature, gapes toward space for the satellite deployment. Then one of the mission specialists activates the system that opens the motorized cover of the sun shield. Nothing happens. A second attempt also fails. Instructors sitting at the console outside have jammed the sun shield shut.

The launch window has already opened when the astronauts call an urgent strategy session with Mission Control. Television cameras are mounted on the shuttle's manipulator arm, and the crew quickly decides to use them, as well as cameras installed in the payload bay, to get a better look at the stubborn sun shield on two television monitors.

The upper screen shows a view of the sun shield and the manipulator arm through the lens of a camera in the aft end of the payload bay. The lower screen is split in half. On the left is another view of the sun shield and manipulator arm; on the right appears a close-up of the sun shield as seen by a camera mounted on the manipulator arm.

A Versatile Bag of Tricks

The computer display reproduced at right is a small sample of the nearly 7,000 difficulties that a simulator instructor can conjure up to challenge astronauts in training. Here the instructor has selected a simulated helium leak. Helium is used to provide pressure for the fuel system supplying the thrusters near the shuttle's nose, which keep the spacecraft pointed in the correct direction. To simulate some problems, the instructor must indicate the magnitude of the difficulty — the rate at which the fuel system is leaking helium, for example. To duplicate other malfunctions, such as the failure of a switch, the instructor transmits a simple "yes" or "no" to the simulator's host computer. Malfunctions are organized by category: navigation troubles, computer gremlins, propulsion fizzles and the like. An instructor can combine individual failures into thousands of scenarios. To make matters worse — and even more realistic — computers simulate chains of problems that would follow as a result of the one the instructor selects.

Near-Failure Averted

With five minutes left before the simulated launch window closes, the mission specialist spots what he believes is the problem. A bent frame has snagged the sun-shield fabric. He calls Mission Control and suggests using the manipulator arm to release the shield. Permission to do so is granted.

The manipulator arm was not designed for this purpose; mispositioning the arm could damage a probe fitted on the end. Gingerly, the mission specialist pushes at the sun shield with the arm, but nothing happens on the first try or the next, half a minute later. On the third attempt, he applies a bit more force — and the sun shield pops open.

Deployment can now proceed. Mounted on a turntable, the satellite is spun at 50 revolutions per minute for stability, then released. Springs shove it out of the payload bay into space, free of the shuttle that brought it there. In 45 minutes or so, the satellite and the shuttle will have drifted a safe distance apart. Only then does a rocket engine ignite, boosting the satellite into its intended orbit.

The instructors sitting at the console have been looking over the astronauts' shoulders during the entire proceeding. Computer monitors in the instructor stations duplicate the information displayed on the instrument panel inside the simulator as well as the views that the astronauts see out the space-shuttle windows.

At the conclusion of the session, instructors and shuttle crew meet for a post-mortem of the flight. Together they discuss what went well and what went poorly with the simulation — and why. Sometimes mistakes can be attributed to the simulator itself, which is then reprogrammed to provide a truer rendition of reality. When the astronauts err, future simulations are planned to polish their performance so that when the time comes to fly a real mission, it will fall solidly in the success column.

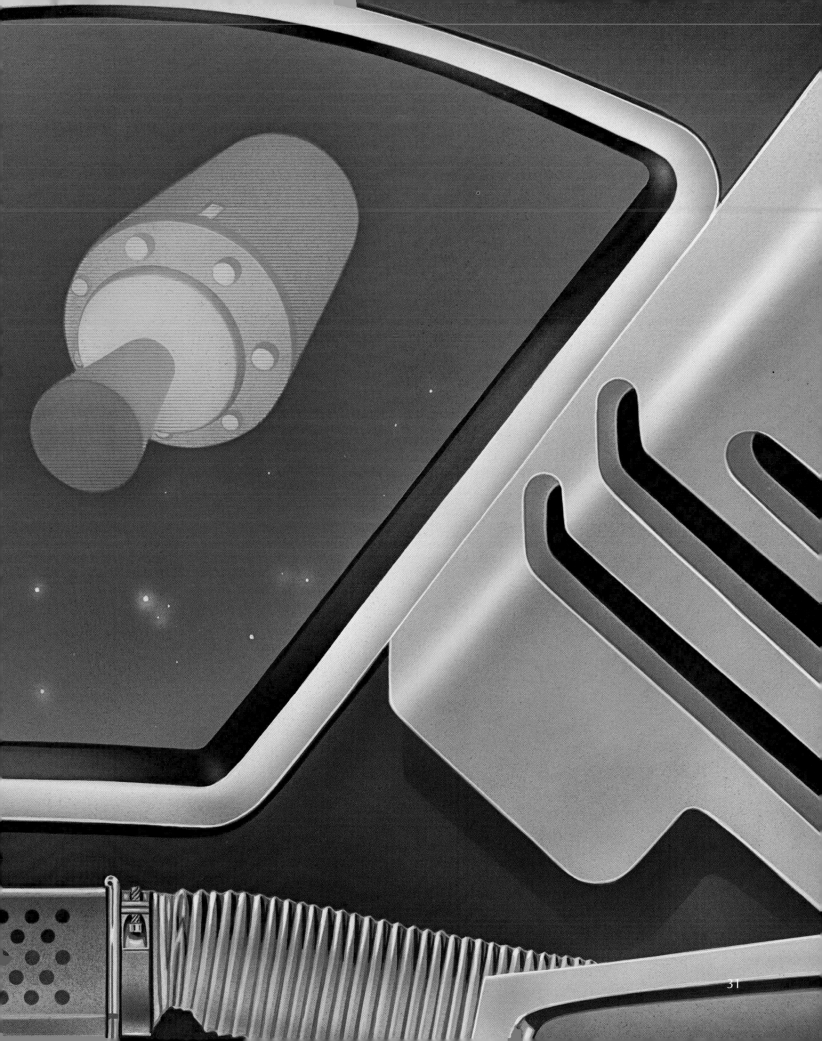

Moonbound

"It was like a blitzkrieg," recalled IBM engineer Leroy Jimerson. "People didn't know what hit them." On Wednesday, March 7, 1962, a teletypewriter came alive at the IBM Electronic Systems Center in Owego, New York, and printed a message from McDonnell Aircraft: ENTER PURCHASE ORDER Y20163R TO PROVIDE THE GEMINI INERTIAL GUIDANCE SYSTEM. Roughly translated, the terse communiqué signaled that McDonnell had hired IBM to build a guidance system similar to those installed in rockets. Though few at the plant had heard much about Project Gemini, IBM "had key personnel assigned and working by Friday," said Jimerson. "By the end of the second week, we were in high gear."

Briefed by McDonnell and NASA representatives, the IBM workers learned that Project Gemini was to be the United States' next manned venture into space, the follow-up to Project Mercury. McDonnell was building the Gemini space-craft; IBM's job was to construct the digital computer that would become the nerve center of the capsule's navigation, guidance and control system.

Until that time, the only computers to fly into space had been those used for rocket guidance. The Gemini computer would be the first general-purpose digital computer aboard a spacecraft. It was to be installed near the crew compartment and would take the place of ground-based data processors in handling guidance and control calculations. For the Gemini astronauts, the computer promised looser bonds to Earth. For IBM, building the device represented a formidable challenge: to shrink technology then found only in large mainframe computers into a machine that would fit inside a space capsule. IBM's John Lenz, an admin-istrator for the project, likened the task to fitting "a refrigerator inside a hatbox."

THE BIRTH OF GEMINI

Project Gemini was a newcomer to America's space program, announced scarcely three months earlier by NASA and shoehorned between the ongoing Mercury program and Project Apollo, the United States' bid to put a man on the moon. Planning for Apollo had been under way for nearly two years, commenc-ing with studies of how best to accomplish a lunar landing.

Initially, many NASA scientists assumed that astronauts would fly to the moon, land and return aboard a single vehicle. This scheme hinged on the construction of a gargantuan rocket booster powerful enough to break free of Earth's gravity while carrying a spacecraft laden with fuel for the return trip. The proposed launch vehicle was an experimental rocket called Nova. Producing 21 million pounds of thrust, it would be almost 60 times as powerful as the Atlas rockets that shot the 4,000-pound Mercury capsules into orbit. But Nova was still on the drawing boards when Apollo got started, and many experts doubted that such a massive rocket could be built before President Kennedy's 10-year deadline for reaching the moon.

One of those skeptics was Wernher von Braun, whose former Peenemünde team had become the nucleus of NASA's new George C. Marshall Space Flight

Center, established in 1960 by transferring part of the army's Redstone Arsenal to the civilian space agency's control. Von Braun's own suggestion was to build a moonship in space. His plan called for launching several smaller rockets, each hoisting part of the spacecraft into Earth orbit, where it would be assembled. Upon its completion, astronauts would be ferried to it from Earth for the moon flight.

A third, dark-horse possibility was a technique called lunar-orbit rendezvous (LOR), an idea almost singlehandedly championed by NASA engineer John Houbolt, who headed a small study group at the agency's Langley Research Center in Hampton, Virginia. LOR called for a mother ship to orbit the moon while a smaller craft descended to the lunar surface and returned. As early as 1916, space-travel visionaries had talked of such a procedure, which would minimize the power and fuel requirements for a lunar landing and takeoff. But upon hearing the suggestion, von Braun simply replied, "No, that's no good." He, like many other experts, considered the idea too complicated — and too hazardous. A missed rendezvous in lunar orbit, beyond the range of assistance from home, could spell death for the astronauts.

By the end of 1961, the direct-ascent scheme had been essentially ruled out: The immense Nova rocket was indeed unlikely to be built in time. This left a choice between using LOR, which Houbolt's persistence had kept alive, and assembling a moonship in Earth orbit. Either plan required the perfection of two unproven and potentially dangerous techniques: rendezvous in orbit and the joining, or docking, of two spacecraft in flight. Furthermore, any lunar excursion would require NASA to prove in advance that astronauts could survive a long journey in space, that they could venture safely outside the protective shell of their spacecraft and that they could navigate without assistance from Earth. While waiting for a final decision, NASA drew up plans to work out these details. NASA named the project Gemini, after the astral twins of the zodiac, to evoke the endeavor's central mission — rendezvous between two spacecraft — and the two-man crews that would carry it out.

Gemini quickly gathered speed. Between April and September of 1962, NASA chose nine new astronauts who, along with three of the veteran Mercury pilots, began preparing for Gemini flights in Houston, Texas, where construction of the sprawling new Manned Space Flight Center had just begun. At McDonnell Aircraft's plant in St. Louis, Missouri, the first Gemini spaceships were being developed; the Martin Marietta Corporation in Baltimore, Maryland, was building the Titan II rockets, which would boost the capsules into orbit. And in Owego, IBM engineers were racing against the clock to have their computer ready by spring.

A CALCULATED SYSTEM FOR NAVIGATION, GUIDANCE AND CONTROL

IBM delivered the first Gemini computer in May 1963. It was a prototype of the final product and not much to look at, recalled astronaut Wally Schirra more than 20 years later. "Imagine a box with a lot of coat hangers bent in all directions," he said. "It was very crude compared to today's computers."

The machine weighed 58 pounds, just one pound less than the limit set by NASA. The assembly fit into an irregularly shaped container about 19 inches long and curved on one side to nestle snugly against the inside wall of the capsule. Arithmetic and logic circuitry consisted of thousands of electronic components — transistors and diodes for the most part — closely packed on layers of interconnecting boards. An epoxy compound cushioned the transistors from shock and protected them against extremes in temperature.

The principal role of the computer was to assist the astronauts in steering the craft. Unlike a Mercury spacecraft, which had virtually no maneuvering ability and followed a path determined by the trajectory of its Atlas booster rocket, the more agile Gemini craft was fitted with a precision orbital maneuvering system, consisting of a battery of thrusters and attitude-control jets at the fingertips of the mission commander. In the simplest terms, the computer's job was to tell the astronauts when and how long to fire these devices in order to steer the capsule.

In profile, a Gemini mission consisted of an accurately guided ascent and orbital insertion, followed by a series of complex orbital maneuvers. Next came a set of smaller, finely tuned movements leading to rendezvous and ultimately to contact with a target vehicle. Later, the capsule returned to Earth. Software was written for each of these phases — as well as for some of the preflight check-out procedures — and the program was divided into five modules: prelaunch, ascent, orbital flight and catch-up, rendezvous, and reentry. The astronauts selected the appropriate module by turning a rotary switch.

The prelaunch software ran a diagnostic routine to check out the computer prior to flight. The ascent software allowed the computer to operate as a backup to the Titan's guidance system, monitoring the booster's velocity and direction and standing by to issue steering commands if the rocket's own radio-controlled system failed.

Once the capsule was in orbit, the computer worked as part of an intricate navigation, guidance and control system that included the spacecraft-tracking network *(pages 15-16)*, headquartered at Goddard Space Flight Center, Maryland, which had been established for Project Mercury. At Mission Control in Houston, an IBM 7094 mainframe computer handled most of the navigation and guidance chores. To determine exactly where the spacecraft was located and where it was headed, Mission Control used tracking information supplied by Goddard to compute the craft's so-called state vector — its velocity and position at a given time. It then used this data in a program called External Delta V — "External" because the program's calculations were performed outside the spacecraft on the ground and "Delta V" after the scientific notation for the changes in velocity prescribed by the software along each of three axes (up-and-down, backward-and-forward, side-to-side) to set the capsule on the correct course.

The results of the Delta V calculations were radioed to the spacecraft, and the pilot entered them on a 10-digit keyboard located on the right side of the instrument panel. The computer, using the orbital-flight module of the software, processed the data and sent the results to an instrument called the Incremental Velocity Indicator (IVI), mounted in front of the flight commander. Consisting of three counters, the IVI displayed, for each axis, the difference between the capsule's current velocity and that needed to accomplish a maneuver. After igniting the thrusters, the commander continued firing until the IVI displays clicked down to zero — a "burn to zero" as it was called.

External Delta V calculations governed most Gemini flight maneuvers, including all of those used by one vehicle to catch up with another. But once the two vehicles were within a few hundred miles of each other, the rendezvous software in the computer aboard the pursuing craft took over. Using tracking information fed to it from an on-board radar system, the computer worked out the remaining velocity and attitude adjustments needed for the final approach.

A similar transfer of computing responsibility from ground to spaceship took place at the end of a flight. The reentry mechanism consisted of retrorockets, which slowed the craft and sent it earthward, and a set of control jets used to steer the ship to its landing point. Shortly before the retrorockets were to be fired, the crew switched the computer to reentry mode. Under the control of this software module, the computer collected data from the craft's inertial measuring unit (IMU), a collection of gyroscopes and accelerometers that sensed changes in attitude and velocity. The timing of retrofire was determined by the computer in Houston, but once the spacecraft entered the atmosphere, the on-board computer began using the IMU data to calculate steering commands.

The computer's memory — which could accommodate all five software modules as well as data entered by the craft's pilot — was a type called core memory. About the size of a small loaf of bread, the memory consisted of 159,744 tiny perforated tablets, or cores, made of ferrite, an easily magnetized compound of iron. Programs and data, expressed in the binary digits, or bits, that computers understand, were loaded into memory by magnetizing the cores in a clockwise or counterclockwise direction: One direction meant a "1"; the opposite direction, a "0." The advantage of this type of memory is that it never forgets. Unlike modern computer memories, in which data exists as electric charges that are immediately lost if the power is cut, the Gemini computer's magnetic memory would not suffer amnesia if the machine were deprived of electricity, a valuable attribute that allowed astronauts to conserve power by shutting off the computer when it was not needed during long sojourns in orbit.

Although NASA retained a policy of having redundant systems wherever possible, the Gemini capsule could not accommodate a backup computer. To reduce the chance that one would ever be needed, IBM put the machines through a grueling round of stress and endurance tests. In Owego, components were heated, chilled and subjected to a vacuum. As Del Babb, IBM's Gemini product manager, commented: "While you get a nice vibration-free environment in space, it's a pretty rough ride getting there." Thus every unit was subjected to a so-called shake table, which rattled the computer hard enough to reproduce the intense vibrations accompanying lift-off.

Computers that survived the test pummeling were then operated in a diagnostic lab, performing dummy missions simulated by an IBM 7094 mainframe. Other simulations could be set up to mimic real missions in progress; in the event of unforeseen problems in space, ground engineers could test possible solutions and, when one was found, advise the astronauts through Mission Control.

While preparing for the first manned Gemini flight, astronaut Gus Grissom visited Owego and put one of the computers through its paces on the simulator. Afterward, he gave a small pep talk, personally thanking the engineers and technicians for their contribution. "Because of you," he declared, "I won't be up in space with my fingers crossed."

ORCHESTRATING AN ORBITAL PAS DE DEUX

On March 23, 1965, after two unmanned tests of the capsule, Grissom and rookie astronaut John Young took *Gemini 3,* playfully nicknamed *Molly Brown* after the never-say-die character of a Broadway musical, on the mission that the veteran Mercury pilot had practiced at Owego. With the first rendezvous mission still nine months away, the computer made its operational debut as a virtual bystander. The flight — three laps around Earth with no maneuvering in orbit — would make few demands on the machine. Its only significant test that day would be to perform the computations for reentry. And even that would be unnecessary; the maneuvers had been planned in advance, based on wind-tunnel tests of the capsule. So uncertain was NASA of the control system's ability to handle a reentry that Grissom and Young were explicitly instructed to ignore the computer's directions if they differed from those derived from the tests.

As it happened, the computer disagreed strongly with the wind-tunnel predictions. So the two astronauts dutifully ignored the computer — and steered *Molly Brown* to a splashdown nearly 60 miles short of their rescue craft. They spent an uncomfortable half hour in the choppy sea before being picked up. Post-flight analysis vindicated the computer. Had Grissom controlled the spacecraft as the computer instructed, he likely would have landed much closer to his target.

But Del Babb and his team at IBM scarcely had time to congratulate themselves before the machine aboard *Gemini 4* embarrassed them in a painfully public display of ineptitude. Late in the third day of a four-day mission, as *Gemini 4* neared the end of its 48th circuit of Earth, something caused the computer's power system to fail. Astronauts James McDivitt and Edward White (who on the first day of the flight had become the first American to walk in space) could not now use the machine to collect the attitude and velocity data needed for a controlled reentry — much less coax any steering instructions out of it. Once *Gemini 4's* retrorockets were fired and the capsule entered the atmosphere, McDivitt steered it according to backup instructions computed earlier on the ground.

From the time of Vanguard *(page 13),* IBM's close association with America's space program had been a source of immense corporate pride. Now, to the computer giant's chagrin, references to the mysterious "computer glitch" were featured prominently in press accounts of the otherwise textbook-perfect mission. The navy recovered the computer and flew it back to an airforce base, where an anxious Babb picked it up. When he reached Owego with the machine, top company executives were waiting for him, demanding to know what had gone wrong. For the next two and a half months, IBM engineers worked feverishly to reproduce the error — "a failure analysis job you'll never see the likes of again," recalled Babb. But the source of the problem remained a mystery, and soon after *Gemini 5's* computer completed a mission with no signs of repeating its sibling's failure, the search was called off.

The next two Gemini computers launched into space dispelled any lingering reservations with a virtuoso performance as orchestrators of space flight's first orbital rendezvous — a December 1965 meeting between *Gemini* 6 and *Gemini* 7. *Gemini 7,* with Frank Borman and James Lovell aboard, lifted off first, on December 4. The two astronauts remained in orbit for the next 13 days, 18 hours and 35 minutes, simulating an Apollo-length mission and setting a space endurance record. Their craft was the target for Walter Schirra and Thomas Stafford, who took off on December 15 in *Gemini* 6.

Gemini 6 had purposely been launched into an orbit below that of *Gemini* 7. Because of the lower orbit — and the physical laws that govern the flight of satellites *(pages 50-55)* — flight commander Schirra and pilot Stafford were circling the globe faster than *Gemini* 7. In a few hours, they would catch up the 1,200 miles by which they trailed their target — and sail by, miles beneath it. Paradoxically, the remedy was to accelerate, because the only way to raise an object into a different orbit is to sling it there through an increase in velocity. But because a higher orbit also reduces speed, the *Gemini* 6 crew had to time their bursts of acceleration so that ultimately they would match their altitude and speed to *Gemini 7's* as they decreased the distance between the spacecraft to a few feet. Schirra described the process as "like a little ballet."

The first part of the celestial *pas de deux* was choreographed by the computer at Houston, which used External Delta V calculations to determine when and where Schirra should fire his thrusters to make the necessary orbital adjustments. Schirra made his first move 94 minutes into the flight, when Mission Control at Houston instructed *Gemini* 6 to increase its velocity by 13 feet per second — about nine miles per hour. Pilot Stafford punched the figures on the computer's keys, and Schirra's IVI displayed the required velocity increases. As the capsule passed over New Orleans, Schirra fired the thrusters for 15 seconds. Two additional velocity corrections during the next few hours brought *Gemini* 6 into radar range of *Gemini* 7, some 270 miles ahead and about 15 miles higher. At this point, Stafford set the computer on rendezvous mode, in which it began using data from the spacecraft's radar to guide the ship in a gentle loop that would bring it nose to nose with *Gemini* 7.

At 2:33 p.m. that day, nearly six hours after launch, Schirra eased his spacecraft in front of *Gemini* 7, perfectly matching his target's speed and direction. The two ships kept in close company for five hours, moving from 300 feet to a handshake's distance apart. At one point, Schirra and Stafford flew in slow circles around Borman and Lovell. Schirra later said he "felt like a terrier playing with a bone." Rendezvous, a crucial maneuver for future missions, had been accomplished with surprising ease.

As the Gemini flights became progressively more complex, computer programs for the missions expanded. By the time of the *Gemini* 7/6 mission in 1965, the software threatened to exceed the core memory available — 39,000 thirteen-bit computer words. In anticipation of this, IBM had contracted with Connecticut's Raymond Engineering Laboratory to build a device called an Auxiliary Tape Memory (ATM), which used a reel of magnetic recording tape to store program modules until they were needed. The 26-pound tape drive had a capacity of 90,000 words, plenty of space to hold whatever programs might be necessary.

The ATM first traveled into space on March 16, 1966, aboard *Gemini* 8. On this flight, astronauts Neil Armstrong and David Scott were to ease the nose of their ship into the docking port fastened to an Agena rocket that had been launched into orbit ahead. That docking came off without a hitch, but half an hour later the Agena rocket and the Gemini capsule, still coupled together, began to spin like a giant centrifuge. Armstrong backed away from the Agena, hoping to halt his twirling spacecraft. But *Gemini 8* tumbled even faster, at the dizzying rate of one revolution per second.

In danger of losing consciousness, Armstrong immediately realized that a thruster had fired unbidden and was steadily accelerating the spin. He shut down power to the malfunctioning jet, then fired one of *Gemini 8's* two sets of reentry control thrusters in a last-ditch attempt to stop the wild spin. The ploy worked, but it exhausted the fuel for those rockets and left Armstrong and Scott with only a backup set. Because it was NASA policy to abort a mission if a critical system was jeopardized, the two astronauts were told to get back to Earth as quickly as possible. In this instance, doing so would land them in the Pacific Ocean instead of in their scheduled Atlantic splashdown area. They turned to the ATM to load the reentry program into the computer. An early model of the device had flunked a laboratory vibration test, and ground controllers waited apprehensively for six minutes while the data was transferred. Despite the spacecraft's earlier gyrations, the transfer went smoothly, and the astronauts were able to use the computer's calculations to help them steer the spacecraft to an emergency landing only seven miles from a rescue ship.

After Armstrong's and Scott's wild ride, Gemini flights continued uneventfully for another year. By November 1966, when *Gemini 12* returned from the project's final mission, the program had more than achieved its objectives. Inside of just two years, America had sent 10 manned spacecraft into Earth orbit, proving the United States to be a strong contender in the space race with the Soviet Union. Extended missions and extravehicular activities (EVA) in space had become almost commonplace. American astronauts had learned to maneuver their spacecraft through the heavens with the confidence of motorists wheeling along a freeway. And the performance of the sturdy little Gemini computer had demonstrated beyond a shadow of a doubt that computers had become a valuable asset to manned space flight.

CHECKING OUT APOLLO

While Gemini had occupied center stage, Project Apollo had been steadily taking shape. Largely due to dogged campaigning by the supremely confident John Houbolt and his supporters at NASA's Langley Research Center ("Give us the go-ahead," wrote Houbolt to NASA headquarters, "and we will put men on the moon in very short order"), lunar-orbit rendezvous had emerged in mid-1962 as the winning method for a moon mission. The dangers of a missed rendezvous remained, but in the end they were overshadowed by the difficulties and expense of building and testing a moonship in Earth orbit, as von Braun's plan demanded. Recognizing the shortcomings of his own approach, the German engineer at last conceded that LOR offered "the highest confidence factor" in getting to the moon quickly. As soon as von Braun capitulated, said Houbolt later, "the last hurdle had been cleared."

Two interconnected vehicles were to be used. One capsule, the command module, would carry a three-man crew into lunar orbit. Attached behind it would be a service module, which would provide the life-support and propulsion apparatus. The second craft, the lunar-landing module, would detach from the front of the command module for the descent to the moon.

Because Apollo astronauts would travel beyond hope of assistance from Earth, planners recognized early on that if anything went amiss, computers aboard the spacecraft would have to be more capable than any yet sent into space. Meanwhile, the very business of getting the spacecraft off the ground was becoming more complex than ever before.

Each of the moonship's two vehicles would contain thousands of components. To ensure their reliability, all of them would have to be tested repeatedly, from the factory floor to the launch pad at Cape Canaveral. For Thomas Walton, the prospect loomed as a nightmare. Walton was an independent-minded test engineer assigned to preflight check-out of the Mercury capsules during the period when plans for Apollo were being made. The space age was dawning, but test procedures had progressed little beyond those used for airplanes. They were "pretty damn primitive," Walton recalled. "We would literally put hundreds of cables through the hatch and hook them up to various things in the spacecraft."

Each wire carried information about a particular spacecraft function to a room where it was displayed as squiggles inked on paper by strip-chart recorders or as movements of needles on gauges and dials. Test engineers compared the readings with tables and charts of correct values to track down any malfunctioning components. During the countdown to lift-off, these painfully slow procedures took place in the hazardous environment of the launch pad with the spacecraft already mated to the booster rocket and its explosive load of fuel.

To Walton, Mercury check-out, with fewer than 100 launch-pad measurements, was bad enough. The thought of applying the same methods to the far more complex Apollo craft—anticipated to require 2,000 such measurements—was appalling. "My God, we can't go on this way," he later remembered saying. "We've got to do something."

TWO SYSTEMS TO CERTIFY A SAFE LAUNCH
As a first step, Walton devised an experimental ground station to process Mercury check-out data with a digital computer instead of the existing battery of gauges and dials. His improvised test center demonstrated to his superiors that engineering data previously shown on gauges and dials was less likely to be misread when displayed as numbers. Furthermore, the computer freed engineers from their charts and tables; it could be programmed to report whether a component had passed a test or failed it.

Given the go-ahead in 1962 to set up an automated check-out system for the Apollo craft, Walton and a colleague, Gary Woods, began a search for suitable equipment. They needed a computer that could handle at least 200,000 logical operations per second — a speed that few computers of the day could achieve. After a detailed survey of the machines available at the time, the two engineers found one fast enough — a minicomputer produced by Control Data Corporation called the CDC 160G. A pair of these machines formed the nucleus of what became known as the acceptance check-out equipment system (ACE). One computer handled the transmission, called the uplink, sending to various spacecraft test-points the commands that simulated typical flight conditions. The other computer handled the downlink; it processed the data returning from the spacecraft and certain other equipment, such as fuel tanks.

Data traveled in both directions through coaxial cables, which can carry multiple transmissions through a single line, thus eliminating the tangle of wires used for Mercury check-out. ACE displayed test results in the form of numbers or letters. If the reading in question fell outside predetermined limits — indicating too much or too little pressure from a fuel pump, for example — the digits would blink repeatedly to attract an engineer's attention.

In late 1965, ACE passed its first major trial at the Cape (renamed Cape Kennedy after the president's assassination in 1963). The occasion was the check-out of an early, unmanned Apollo spacecraft. The success had been anticipated. Even as Walton and Woods were establishing Cape Kennedy's ACE system, they oversaw the installation of 14 additional ACE stations to handle tests and check-out at factories in California, New York and Texas, where Apollo's command, service and lunar-landing modules were taking shape.

Meanwhile, a separate system was under development for preflight testing of the massive three-stage Saturn V booster rockets being built for Project Apollo by Wernher von Braun's engineers at Marshall Space Flight Center. The task of checking out the boosters promised to be even more daunting than that of testing the spacecraft: The rocket was expected to contain some 5,000 test-points. Engineers estimated that, using Project Mercury procedures, certifying a Saturn safe for launch would take more than a year.

In September 1961, Ludie Richard, director of systems engineering at Marshall, put forward a novel proposal: enlist the rocket's on-board guidance computer to help approve the booster for launch. Once, such an idea would have been laughably impractical. Rocket guidance computers, descended from the analog devices pioneered in Germany during World War II, had been considerably refined over the years by American rocket experts, but analog computers shared an inherent limitation. Built to perform one task, an analog machine could not undertake a different one unless its circuitry was redesigned. Thus, transforming a traditional guidance computer into a testing computer would have been virtually impossible. Doing so would have meant building a new machine.

Digital computers, however, can be made to perform different jobs merely by altering their software. Accordingly, analog guidance computers were being phased out in favor of the more versatile digital variety. For the Saturn, IBM was building an extraordinarily capable device called the launch vehicle digital computer (LVDC), which would dramatically expand the role of guidance devices. In its final configuration, the LVDC would manage the rocket's entire flight, from igniting the engines to guiding the spent third stage safely away from Apollo once the ship was on its way to the moon.

Richard's idea was to incorporate the LVDC into an automated check-out procedure by writing software that would instruct the guidance computer to monitor sensors at various test-points on the rocket. It would then pass these results to a digital computer stationed on the Saturn launcher, a mobile structure on which the rocket was assembled and later transported to the launch pad. The data would be transferred to a third computer, manned by test engineers in the launch control room. For the latter two computers, Richard proposed the RCA 110, an off-the-shelf machine of proven reliability that had already seen wide service as a controller of equipment in rugged environments such as electric-generating plants and steel mills.

By 1963, Richard's engineers had settled most of the details for a new Saturn launch control and check-out system. The LVDC would be responsible for checking the rocket guidance and control systems that it would later operate in flight. The RCA 110 on the launcher would control and monitor these tests; it would also be responsible for checking other rocket systems that were crucial to a successful flight. The second RCA computer would permit test engineers to send commands and requests for information to the launch-site computer during the last five hours of the countdown, when only astronauts and their small team of support personnel were allowed near the rocket. Data would shuttle to and from the three computers over high-speed cables; those running, umbilical-like, from the rocket to the RCA 110 on the launch pad would be automatically jerked free just before takeoff. The system would be able to monitor 150,000 test signals per minute and not only indicate that a problem existed but give information about its nature and causes.

Richard had to move diplomatically to implement the system, in part because of resistance from test engineers at the Cape. Knowing little about computers, some engineers feared that programmers and humming ranks of gray-enameled boxes might replace them. Others suspected that a complex computerized system was inherently unreliable. Yet their good will was essential to the success of the project. Although test people were short on computer knowledge, programmers knew even less about check-out procedures and would count on cooperation from the engineers to make the software function correctly.

A key step in dissipating this cloud of suspicion occurred at Huntsville in 1963, with the introduction of a new computer language called ATOLL — acceptance, test or launch language. Until then, all check-out and guidance instructions had been written by programmers in difficult-to-learn assembly language, a rudimentary form of notation not far removed from the binary digits manipulated by computers. ATOLL was a variety of engineering shorthand, developed by NASA and IBM software experts, that allowed test engineers to write their own computer software. The new language not only removed the roadblock posed by assembly language, it provided a common tongue for engineers at Saturn manufacturing facilities, where test programs for rocket components had been written in a babel of a half dozen languages. Through the hands-on experience with computers that NASA engineers gained through ATOLL, they were increasingly won over to these remarkable machines. By July 1965, well before the first Apollo mission was scheduled, about half the prelaunch check-out procedures had been computerized.

BLOCK-BY-BLOCK: BUILDING APOLLO'S COMPUTER

By this time, the navigation and control system that would guide Apollo missions to the moon and back should also have been nearly ready. But it was not, and only a genuine miracle seemed likely to complete the work in time.

Work on the system had started in 1961, even before IBM had been hired to build the on-board computer for Project Gemini. The man in charge of developing the computer and other components of the moonship's guidance and navigation system was Milton Trageser, a veteran engineer at the Massachusetts Institute of Technology's prestigious Instrumentation Laboratory. NASA gave M.I.T. the job largely on the basis of a prospectus — written during early planning stages for the project — that outlined a guidance system that could find the moon on the trip out and Earth on the trip back.

M.I.T.'s assignment was widely regarded as the most ambitious undertaking in aerospace computer technology to date. Trageser and his staff faced the task of creating, virtually from scratch, a fully computerized celestial navigation system. It was to consist of three elements: an inertial measuring unit to sense changes in attitude and velocity; an optical instrument to take bearings on Earth, moon and stars; and a digital computer to control the system. The various components were to be designed at M.I.T. and then built by industrial contractors.

The computer was the tough nut to crack. Designing it was greatly complicated by NASA's desire for an autonomous system that would have no help at all from computers on the ground. One reason was political: In the early 1960s, a handful of U.S. officials feared that the Soviet Union might attempt to disrupt communications to and from American spacecraft. A more compelling and practical reason for a self-sufficient computer seemed to be that in orbiting the moon before a landing and afterward, Apollo would fly on the dark side, out of touch with Earth, for half an hour at a time. Furthermore, to send telemetry from the moonship in lunar orbit and receive a reply from computers on Earth would take two and a half seconds, an interminable delay for the astronauts, who might have to make split-second decisions under circumstances that no one could foresee.

The feasibility of an independent computer was hotly debated. NASA administrator James Webb openly voiced his concern that M.I.T. could not come up with a workable system by decade's end. Charles Stark Draper, a pilot and engineer with more than 30 years' experience in designing aerospace instruments and the director of the Instrumentation Lab, asserted tartly that he was so confident of success he would be willing to make the voyage and run the system himself. "Let me know what application blanks I should fill out," he wrote to an amused NASA. As to concerns about the guidance system being ready on time, Draper vowed: "You'll have it when you need it."

But Webb had good cause for misgivings. Not only was the project one of unprecedented complexity, but NASA, still a year away from settling on the lunar-orbit rendezvous method for reaching the moon, provided almost no guidelines for the job. M.I.T. engineer Eldon Hall recalled that the lab was given only one order: "Figure out how to get to the moon and back safely." Years later he observed that if a complete set of specifications had been available in 1961, no one would have thought a solution possible.

Hall headed the M.I.T. team that had earlier built a digital guidance computer for the navy's Polaris missile. His group moved almost intact to the Apollo project. They submitted their first design, dubbed Block I, in 1962 — just after NASA settled on lunar-orbit rendezvous as the means for reaching the moon. The decision dramatically increased the burdens on the guidance and navigation system. Two computers would now be needed, one for the command module (CM) and another for the lunar module (LM); and each would require different software that promised to be lengthier and far more complex than originally envisioned.

The LM's needs were the most difficult to meet. The squat little vehicle was inherently unstable and could not be controlled by an unaided human pilot. Only a computer, with its high-speed processing power, could calculate and initiate the constant stream of rapid-fire adjustments needed to keep the craft under control and land it safely on the moon.

The Block I computer was not up to the job. It had too little memory for the necessary software. Moreover, it lacked the special circuits that would enable it to receive information from both the LM's radar and the inertial measuring devices and to send instructions to the vehicle's engine and attitude-control system. The Block I design was relegated to a secondary role in the Apollo program — as the command module computer for early tests of the spacecraft in Earth orbit. Hall's group returned to their drawing boards to come up with a computer for both the command ship and the lander for the lunar missions.

Block II, a new design submitted in early 1964, appeared to be a winner. In remaking the computer, Hall and his engineers provided the necessary interfaces for the LM and employed state-of-the-art integrated circuits in the processing units. Integrated circuits, which package entire computer functions as single components, were still in their infancy in the early 1960s. But M.I.T. had convinced NASA that their advantages — compactness, speed and low power consumption — far outweighed any risks the space agency typically associated with computer technology's leading edge. The gamble paid off handsomely: When the Block II computer was completed in 1965, it was smaller and lighter than its predecessor and it required less power. It could also execute many types of computations faster.

The engineers also doubled the computer's memory. As in Block I, memory consisted of two types of magnetic cores. A small area of erasable memory — temporary storage where data was processed during missions — was similar to that used in the Gemini computer. This section could hold 2,000 sixteen-bit words. The much larger section, 36,000 sixteen-bit words of permanent storage reserved for Apollo's programs, was called core-rope memory. It differed from the erasable core memory in the way that thin copper wires were threaded through the tiny, doughnut-shaped cores. A wire strung directly through a hole stored as "1"; bypassing a hole created a "0." This created a kind of electronic tapestry in which Apollo programs were set indelibly into memory by the pattern of the weave, immune to power surges or other external influence short of physical damage to the components.

By 1966, as time for the first Apollo test flights approached, the Apollo computer was coming along nicely. But a computer without software is as useless as an army without a commander, and the moon-mission programs were nowhere near ready to be woven into the computer's memory.

APOLLO SOFTWARE

In the absence of guidelines from NASA, M.I.T.'s Apollo software group started by adapting guidance programs that had been written for the Polaris missile and for an unmanned Mars probe designed in the late 1950s but never built. With the decision for lunar-orbit rendezvous, the software requirements increased dramatically. Different programs now had to be written for the command module and the landing module, for Blocks I and II, and for the Earth-orbit exercises and the lunar missions. Initially, M.I.T. had figured that 15 to 20 software engineers could easily write all of the necessary programs; by the mid-1960s, more than 300 programmers were churning out Apollo code. After nearly five years' effort, much of the software written for Block I had not been thoroughly tested, and programming for Block II exceeded the available memory by some 30 percent.

From the outset, NASA had left software development entirely in the Instrumentation Lab's hands. But in March 1966, NASA appointed Bill Tindall as software watchdog to the Apollo project. Tindall, who as a computer tyro in 1960 had been placed in charge of software development for the Mercury tracking network, had since then been planning Gemini missions at NASA's Real Time Computing Center in Houston. He was appalled at the confusion and lack of direction he found at M.I.T. Commuting weekly to Boston, he wrote a succession of blunt memos documenting M.I.T.'s software woes in sobering detail. The grim message of the acerbic "Tindallgrams," as they became known, was that the troubled software effort had become the crucial pacing item for Apollo flights. At M.I.T., Tindall's arrival came as an unwelcome intrusion, and morale plummeted.

On Friday the 13th of May, a day that M.I.T. participants would later recall as Black Friday, Tindall presided over a stormy and traumatic meeting in which entirely new software specifications were hammered out and the whole philosophy of Apollo missions was revised.

"That day it was established that total autonomy would just not work," said Tindall of the conference. "There wasn't enough memory, and besides, it was totally unnecessary." Tindall's experience with Gemini had convinced him that numerous Apollo navigation and guidance chores — midcourse corrections en route to the moon, for example — could be computed more easily on Earth using

External Delta V programs. The delay in transmission time no longer loomed as a barrier; even orbital maneuvers on the far side of the moon could be computed in Houston and the results transmitted to the astronauts before they passed from view. And any cold-war paranoia about interference from America's Soviet space-race competitors had long since vanished: "The craziest thing I've ever heard," snorted Tindall years later.

NASA's insistence on complete spacecraft independence, the rationale behind much of the software that had been written over the preceding years, dissolved instantly, and many on the M.I.T. staff saw months of work go down the drain as entire programs were struck from the roster. A host of guidance and navigation functions were taken over by computers at Houston, and from Black Friday onward, NASA managers kept a close eye on the programming. A software control board was set up to review every modification. As one space agency official put it, M.I.T. "could not change a single bit without permission."

But Apollo's software ills could not be cured overnight, and bugs lurked in every major program. A potentially serious one was uncovered in January 1967, less than a month before the first scheduled Apollo launch — a manned orbital test flight of the command module. A simulation of the reentry program revealed a 138-second discrepancy for retrorocket ignition time between the calculations made by the on-board software and those from the software on the ground. It was too late to alter the program; the core rope that contained it had already been installed in the spacecraft. Rather than scrub the mission, NASA decided to transmit commands generated by the Mission Control computers at Houston to the astronauts who would manually key the numbers into the Apollo computer, overriding the faulty software.

Tragically, the opportunity to employ the improvised solution never materialized. On January 27, 1967, the *Apollo 1* crew — Gus Grissom, Edward White and Roger Chaffee — slid into the command module for a simulated countdown. A fire erupted in the sealed cockpit and raged ferociously in the oxygen-rich atmosphere. All three astronauts were incinerated.

Badly shaken, NASA scrapped the Apollo timetable and embarked on an anguished reappraisal of the project. Every system aboard the Apollo spacecraft and every software module was examined with renewed intensity. For the next two years, Apollo programs were run day and night on a pair of IBM 360-75s — among the fastest computers then available — in simulations designed to ruthlessly root out bugs. By the time manned Apollo flights resumed — after three unmanned test shots between November 1967 and April 1968 — the guidance system and its computers had been developed to a point where impromptu solutions to software problems, like the one that was proposed for *Apollo 1*, were unnecessary.

THE TRIP TO TRANQUILLITY

Apollo's guidance computer — the AGC as it was officially designated — and its software were at last carried into space aboard a manned spaceship in October 1968, when *Apollo 7* orbited Earth to test the revamped command module. Two months later, *Apollo 8* took a Christmas cruise around the moon, dipping to within 60 miles of its cratered surface. The following March, *Apollo 9* carried the lunar module and its computer into space for the first time, and the LM was maneuvered in Earth orbit. Then in May, *Apollo 10,* with the LM coupled to the command ship, flew to the moon. While in orbit there, the LM performed all the maneuvers expected of it save one — an actual landing on the lunar surface.

The navigation, guidance and control system used for these early Apollo missions bore scant resemblance to the autonomous system that had been envisioned in 1961, but the Apollo guidance computers aboard the command module and the LM each managed a more varied set of control and data-processing functions than had been anticipated. The command-module computer handled all of the on-board guidance chores, generating steering commands and aligning the inertial measuring unit in collaboration with the computers in Houston. The computer aboard the LM functioned almost as an additional crew member — a digital auto-pilot that rapidly juggled data from the radar and inertial measuring unit with astronauts' commands to control the craft. Because the LM could not be flown without the aid of an on-board computer, the lander carried a backup machine, built by TRW, called the abort guidance system. Its sole function was to get the lunar module back to the command module if the primary computer failed.

Astronauts communicated with the computers through a display and keyboard unit called the DSKY (pronounced DISK-ey). Using a primitive, numerical language, the crew could issue any of 100 commands to the computer by entering pairs of numbers — from 00 to 99 — that corresponded to instructions such as "display velocity" or "load program." Although rehearsals for the mission had made the astronauts thoroughly familiar with most DSKY instructions, the crew invariably pasted critical information on cue cards. "We had little bits of paper stuck up all over both of those cabins," laughed *Apollo 10's* John Young, describing the apparent chaos inside the command module and the LM during his May 1969 flight.

Two months later, on July 16, 1969, *Apollo 11* lifted off from Cape Kennedy, bearing Young's colleagues Neil Armstrong, Buzz Aldrin and Michael Collins on the journey that would bring to fruition the dreams of centuries, and the herculean technological efforts of a decade. On July 20, the lunar module *Eagle* separated from the command ship *Columbia* and carried Armstrong and Aldrin off on the final leg of the voyage. A landing on the moon was just seven minutes away when alarm lights began to flash on the DSKY in the *Eagle's* cabin. For a few confused seconds, it seemed that the mission might be in danger. But almost instantly, mission controllers in Houston, who were intimately familiar with the computer system, realized that the same situation had occurred in a simulation of the mission several weeks earlier. The lunar module's rendezvous radar, which would later be used to return to the command module, was turned on at this stage of the flight because of a flaw in the mission plan. It made so many requests of the computer that the processor was overloaded. The unsettling alarm lights were the computer's signals that it was eliminating low-priority tasks from the list awaiting processing. There was no danger to the astronauts, and Mission Control assured Armstrong and Aldrin that the lunar-landing module was still Go for landing.

But the distracting interruptions kept the astronauts' eyes glued to their cabin displays, preventing them from carefully perusing the approaching landscape. When Armstrong at last looked out his window, 2,000 feet up and three minutes from landing, he saw he was heading toward a crater the size of a football field, strewn with rocks and boulders. Just in time, the 39-year-old mission commander deftly steered the *Eagle* to a safe, smooth area. "Tranquillity Base here," Armstrong announced. "The *Eagle* has landed." At 4:17 p.m. eastern daylight time, July 20, 1969, humans had arrived on another world.

WINDING DOWN

The computer-generated scare that briefly marred the moon landing was largely forgotten in the euphoria that followed, but its significance was not lost on computer experts outside the space agency. In October 1969, a story in a respected industry magazine criticized the Apollo guidance computer as too slow to do the job it was designed for. The article named a number of commercially available minicomputers that were at least 10 times faster than the AGC and thus could have easily handled the barrage of processing chores that had briefly threatened to overwhelm M.I.T.'s custom-built machine.

The observation was a precursor of criticism that would be periodically leveled at the space program in years to come. Because NASA missions had to be mapped out years before they actually took place, their computer systems, designed at the planning stage, were inevitably rendered obsolete by advancing technology. Typically, both the Gemini and Apollo computers were well behind the state of the art by the time they finally flew. By contemporary standards they seem prehistoric: A personal computer available in the mid-1980s for $1,000 has more than 20 times the memory and 10 times the processing speed of these early spaceborne computers.

But while they may have been behind the technological cutting edge, both computers were consistently reliable, winning the trust of the astronauts and justifying NASA's conservative design policy. The Apollo computer continued to serve for years to come, accompanying men to the moon on five more occasions in the 41 months that followed *Apollo 11's* epoch-making flight. And thereafter, no humans would travel into space without a computer at their side.

The Route to Other Worlds

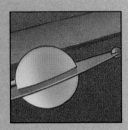

2

When seafarers of earlier eras ventured beyond sight of land, they relied on their knowledge of winds, currents and the heavens to reach distant ports. Today's sea is the void of space, where the need for accurate navigation is just as pressing — and the task of achieving it vastly more complicated. Magellan might never have found his way around the world if the world's land masses behaved like objects in space: Continents and islands would spin as they moved rapidly across the face of the globe, and they would exert an attractive force on each other, as well as on the explorer's vessel.

The problems of navigating in space demand computers capable of performing, in split seconds, calculations that would take years to do by hand. Such computers must be able to determine the spacecraft's position and heading from sightings of the sun, Earth or stars; select the trajectory that will conduct the craft to its destination with a minimum expenditure of fuel; and keep the craft oriented so that antennas and other devices can be pointed in specific directions. It is no exaggeration to say that the development of computers has been as important to the progress of space travel as the development of rockets.

The following pages trace a hypothetical journey from Earth to a space station in Earth orbit and onward to the moon and then Mars. To make the trip would require many months, and a properly outfitted ship might weigh hundreds of tons, which is far too much for launching directly from Earth. So a smaller vehicle, a ferry of sorts, would be used to shuttle components of the ship — including banks of computers — to the space station for assembly in orbit. Once assembled, the interplanetary vessel would be available to take passengers between Mars and Earth, with a stop in lunar orbit to pick up travelers based on the moon.

Coping with Celestial Mechanics

Planets in the solar system (only Mercury, Venus, Earth and Mars appear in this drawing) circle the sun in slightly different orbital planes, exaggerated here for clarity. The orbit of Mars, for example, is inclined about 1.8 degrees to the ecliptic, the plane containing Earth's orbit. The moon's orbit is inclined about five degrees to the ecliptic.

Seen from above *(box, bottom right)*, motion in the solar system is generally counterclockwise. The planets revolve around the sun in a counterclockwise direction; the sun and most of the planets rotate counterclockwise on their axes. Similarly, the moon orbits Earth in a counterclockwise fashion, rotating on its axis in the same direction.

To calculate a course to the moon or to another planet, spacecraft computers must consider the orbit and rotation not only of the starting point — Earth — but also of the destination. Described by the laws of celestial mechanics, these motions take the form of complicated equations. Solving them, a task

Mercury

Venus

to which computers are particularly well suited, enables predicting future positions of celestial bodies so that spacecraft can achieve an interception. Accuracy is essential: An error no larger than a fraction of a degree in aiming a spacecraft from Earth can, if left uncorrected, cause the vehicle to miss a distant planet by hundreds of thousands of miles.

Whether a spacecraft's destination is an outpost in Earth orbit or a neighboring planet circling the sun, certain orbital characteristics apply. The path of an orbit, for example, may be described as forming part of a plane, the two-dimensional surface familiar from high-school geometry. All of the planets revolve around the sun in slightly different orbital planes, each passing through the center of the sun. In addition, the planets travel at different speeds and take varying lengths of time to complete a single revolution, depending on their distance from the sun. The same rules apply to objects orbiting Earth or any other planet.

Because Earth, its moon and the planets all move in different orbital planes, a spacecraft traveling between these objects must change from one plane to another en route. Besides requiring large amounts of fuel, such maneuvers complicate the calculation of spacecraft trajectories.

Earth

Moon

Mars

Destination Mars

The best route in space is rarely the shortest. To move in a straight line between planets generally requires great quantities of fuel to overcome gravity. Instead, spacecraft take advantage of the natural motions of the planets and their satellites. The map at right summarizes a journey from Earth to Mars. First, a space ferry is launched into Earth orbit for rendezvous with a space station. There, the crew and passengers transfer to a long-distance spacecraft, which pauses briefly in moon orbit to take on other travelers bound for Mars.

Timing is a critical factor in these maneuvers. Just as a sharpshooter must lead a moving target and fire while the quarry is within range, a spacecraft must be aimed ahead of its destination in order to arrive there, and the vehicle must take off within a narrow span of time called a launch window. To conserve fuel on the leg to Mars — and because of that planet's orbit relative to Earth's — the interplanetary craft follows a course that will converge with its destination on the far side of the sun, after an eight-month voyage of approximately 360 million miles. The launch window for this trip lasts about a week — and occurs only once every two years.

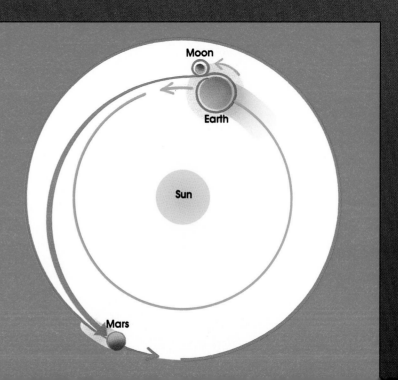

Moon

Earth

Sun

Mars

The Departure from Earth

Rocketing a ferry to a space station in Earth orbit, the first stop on the hypothetical trip to Mars, requires a prodigious amount of fuel. Ferry launches must be carefully planned to minimize the weight of fuel needed and to allow the spacecraft to carry a maximum of passengers and cargo. One way to conserve fuel during launch is to take advantage of Earth's rotation on its axis. Because the planet turns from west to east, a rocket launched in an easterly direction will get a boost into orbit. The effect is like jumping off a revolving merry-go-round. A leap in the direction that the merry-go-round is turning results in a higher speed than a jump the other way. Additional fuel is saved by timing the countdown so that the ferry is launched into the same orbital plane as the space station (*right, top*).

Once aloft and maneuvering toward the space station (*pages 54-55*), the ferry must maintain a specific orientation, or attitude. This delicate task is accomplished through a partnership between the vehicle's on-board computers and a complicated instrument that employs gyroscopes, cousins to a simple childhood toy — a spinning top.

When an object is set awhirl, it exhibits a reluctance to change its axis of rotation. This law of physics explains why a spinning top will balance on its point and why gyroscopes, combined into a device called an inertial measurement unit (IMU), can provide the information necessary to keep a spacecraft properly aligned for docking and for other maneuvers (*right, bottom*).

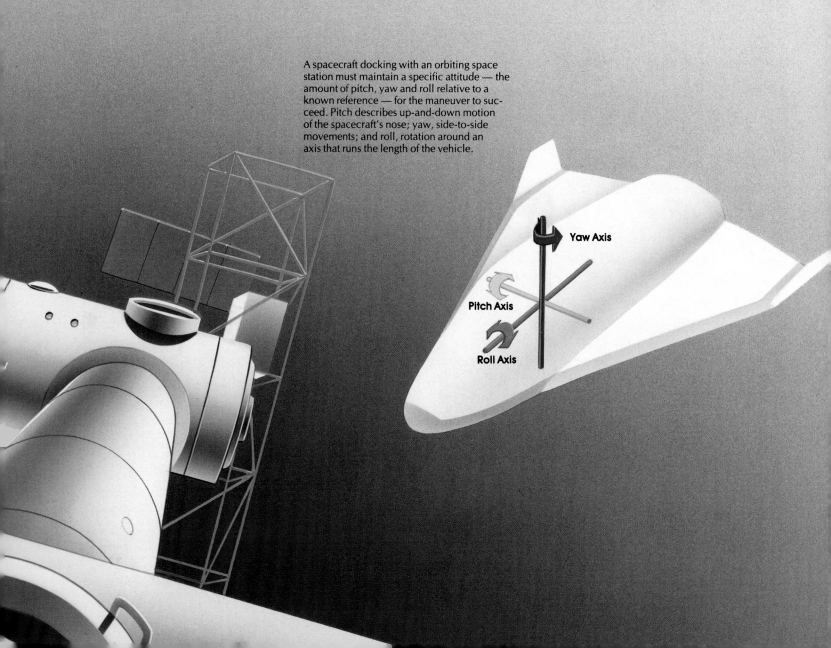

A spacecraft docking with an orbiting space station must maintain a specific attitude — the amount of pitch, yaw and roll relative to a known reference — for the maneuver to succeed. Pitch describes up-and-down motion of the spacecraft's nose; yaw, side-to-side movements; and roll, rotation around an axis that runs the length of the vehicle.

Yaw Axis

Pitch Axis

Roll Axis

Launching into Earth Orbit

A spacecraft launched due east from Cape Canaveral takes full advantage of Earth's counterclockwise rotation to rendezvous with the space station, whose orbit is shown at right. As the station circles the globe along this path, Earth's rotation below carries the Cape out of the orbital plane. A day later — and once a day thereafter — the Florida launch facility passes through the space station's orbital plane, providing the most fuel-efficient opportunity for launching other ferries. In practice, there is a launch window of several minutes during which the difference between the orbital plane of the target space station and that of the chase vehicle is small enough to be bridged.

Maintaining the Proper Attitude

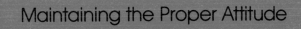

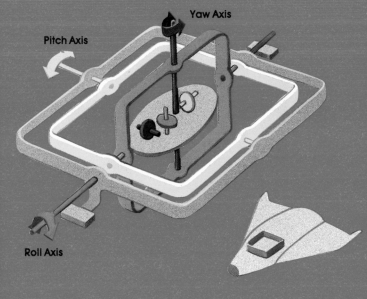

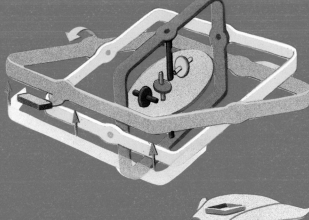

On the level. In an inertial measurement unit, three gyroscopes are part of a system that steadies an oval platform to serve as a reference point for changes in the vehicle's attitude. The platform is mounted in a gimbal framework, which keeps it from tilting. Attached to the spacecraft, the gimbals transmit to the platform the slightest pitching, rolling and yawing motions of the spacecraft. This diagram shows the relationship of the platform to the gimbals when the craft is flying straight and level.

Sensing pitch. Should the nose of the ship rise, the gimbal attached to the vehicle follows *(gray)*. As the gimbal begins to move, it tilts the platform. The pitch gyro *(yellow)*, which resists the attempt to change its axis of rotation, generates a signal that activates electric motors to move the pitch gimbal, restoring the gyro to its original axis of rotation and thereby keeping the platform stable. A sensor notes the gimbal movement and passes the information to a computer, which can then either send instructions to fire small thrusters and return the ship to its original orientation or use the data in other navigational calculations.

The Fine Art of Rendezvous

To rendezvous with a space station that is in Earth orbit, a ferry could, theoretically, take the direct approach, reaching the space station in a single bound, or it could approach its destination more gingerly, taking several steps. In practice, for reasons of safety and economy, the multistep approach is preferred.

On this Mars trip, the ferry from Cape Canaveral is first established in an elliptical, or oval, orbit. Initially, the ferry's orbit does not match the shape of the space station's nearly circular path around Earth. In addition, the ferry orbits at a lower altitude than the space station and thus at a faster speed. (Even though a vehicle must be accelerated to move from a low orbit into a higher one, the velocity needed to maintain an object in orbit is less for higher altitudes than for lower ones.) To complicate matters further, as the ferry's eccentric orbit carries it nearer Earth and then farther away, the effect of gravity on the vehicle varies. Only computers can analyze the situation quickly enough to choreograph a sequence of steps that allows the ferry to rendezvous with its target.

As difficult as the mathematics of orbital mechanics may be, the principle of making circular orbits from elliptical ones is a simple one. The essence of the matter is this: The diameter of a circular orbit around Earth — or any other celestial body — depends only on the satellite's speed. Thus, transforming an elliptical orbit into a circular one requires only that the satellite achieve the speed associated with the altitude of the orbit desired.

An elliptical orbit offers two fuel-efficient opportunities for a satellite (in this case, the Cape Canaveral ferry) to be established in a circular path around its focus (Earth). One occurs at perigee, the point of closest approach to the focus and where a satellite, having moved "downhill" toward Earth, is traveling its fastest (below, left); the other occurs at apogee, the point at which the satellite is farthest from the orbit's focus and traveling its slowest (below, center). Conversely, a circular orbit can be made elliptical by either increasing or decreasing the vehicle's speed (below, right). Repeated application of these principles according to a carefully planned schedule makes it possible not only for the ferry to rendezvous with the space station (right) but for an interplanetary spaceship to reach the moon and continue to Mars (pages 56-57).

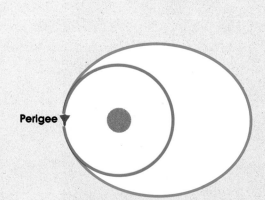

A circular path at perigee. In an elliptical orbit (blue), a satellite's speed at its closest approach to Earth is greater than the velocity for a circular orbit having the same altitude. To establish the vehicle in a circular orbit there, rockets are fired as the satellite approaches perigee, slowing the vehicle from its maximum speed to the velocity required for the new orbit (red).

A circular path at apogee. At a satellite's farthest distance from Earth, its speed is less than required for a circular orbit at that altitude, so it falls toward the planet, accelerating as it approaches perigee. Thus, to establish a satellite in a circular orbit at apogee, rockets accelerate to the speed required for a circular orbit at that height.

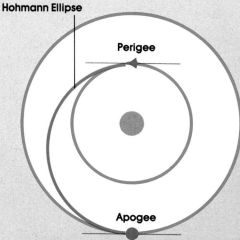

Switching orbits. The most fuel-efficient trajectory from a low circular orbit to a higher one in the same orbital plane is known as a Hohmann transfer ellipse. First, in a reversal of the process shown at far left, speed is increased to produce an elliptical orbit with the perigee equal to the lower altitude and the apogee equal to the higher altitude sought. To enter the larger circular orbit, velocity is again increased when the craft reaches apogee to make up the speed lost as the vehicle moved "uphill" to the higher orbit.

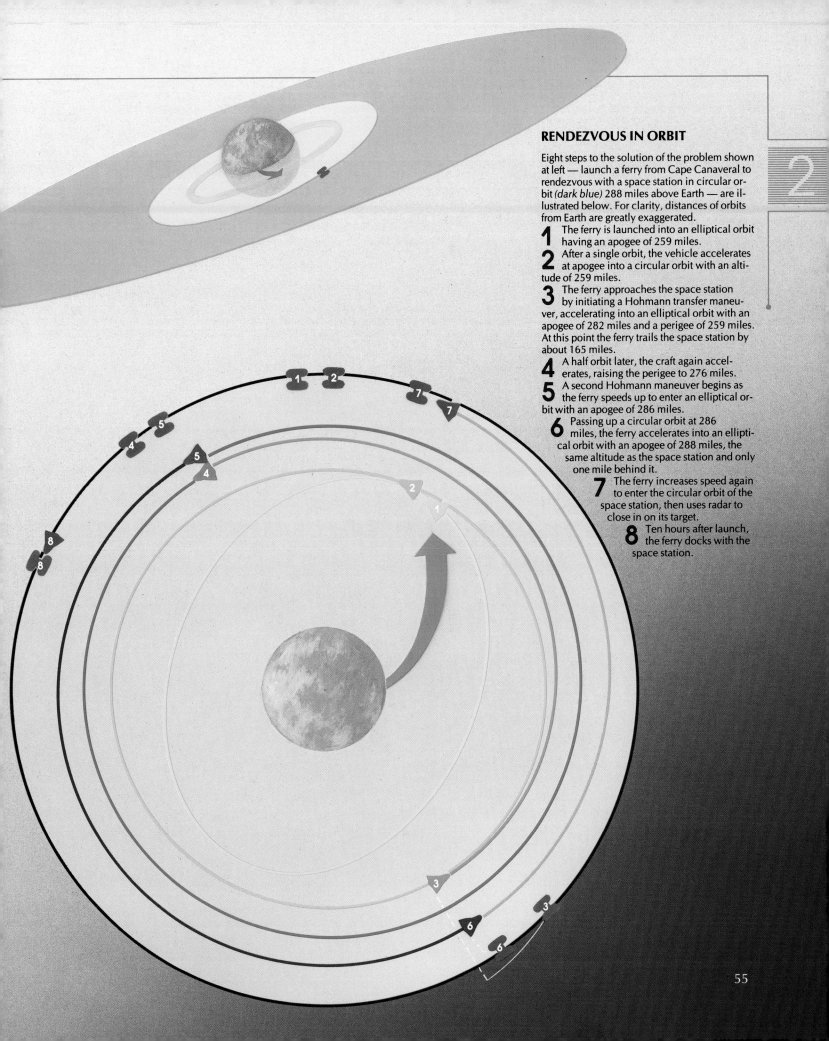

RENDEZVOUS IN ORBIT

Eight steps to the solution of the problem shown at left — launch a ferry from Cape Canaveral to rendezvous with a space station in circular orbit *(dark blue)* 288 miles above Earth — are illustrated below. For clarity, distances of orbits from Earth are greatly exaggerated.

1 The ferry is launched into an elliptical orbit having an apogee of 259 miles.

2 After a single orbit, the vehicle accelerates at apogee into a circular orbit with an altitude of 259 miles.

3 The ferry approaches the space station by initiating a Hohmann transfer maneuver, accelerating into an elliptical orbit with an apogee of 282 miles and a perigee of 259 miles. At this point the ferry trails the space station by about 165 miles.

4 A half orbit later, the craft again accelerates, raising the perigee to 276 miles.

5 A second Hohmann maneuver begins as the ferry speeds up to enter an elliptical orbit with an apogee of 286 miles.

6 Passing up a circular orbit at 286 miles, the ferry accelerates into an elliptical orbit with an apogee of 288 miles, the same altitude as the space station and only one mile behind it.

7 The ferry increases speed again to enter the circular orbit of the space station, then uses radar to close in on its target.

8 Ten hours after launch, the ferry docks with the space station.

Maneuvers in the Third Dimension

The orbital planes of the moon and a space station launched from Cape Canaveral would coincide only for a brief period every 18 years or so. Thus, when a spacecraft departs Earth orbit for the moon, it must first slip from the orbital plane of the space station into the orbital plane of the moon.

This maneuver, essential before the craft can perform a Hohmann transfer to reach the moon — and again before it can repeat the technique to reach Mars — is costly in fuel. But

The diagram below, which illustrates the angle between the orbital plane of the space station (blue) and the orbital plane of the moon (violet), shows how the distance between orbital planes — and the fuel required to bridge it — increases as the spaceship moves away from the node.

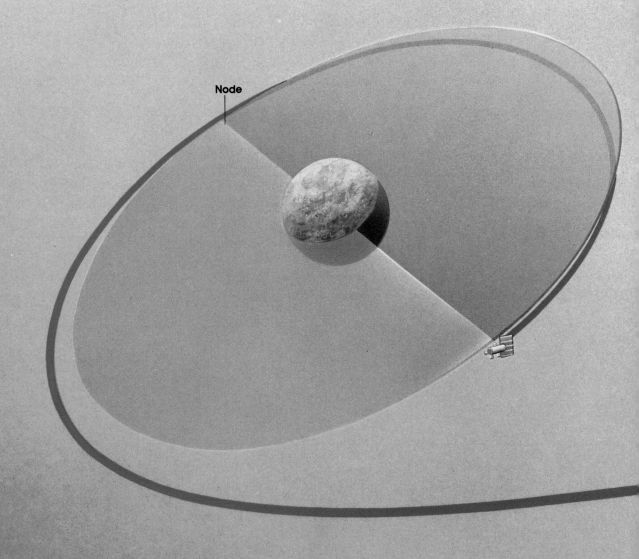

Node

by using computers to compare alternative trajectories and to time the application of thrust, fuel requirements can be minimized. The most fuel-efficient opportunities to move from one orbital plane to another occur where two planes intersect, points known as nodes. The farther from a node the maneuver is attempted, the more the planes have diverged and the greater the amount of fuel required.

In the example shown below, half an orbit after the space-ship switches to the moon's orbital plane, thrusters initiate a Hohmann transfer ellipse timed to allow the craft to intercept the moon. At a space station in moon orbit, passengers then board the interplanetary craft, which will transfer from the plane of the moon's orbit around the sun to that of Mars around the sun *(pages 50-51)*. Only then will the vessel depart for Mars along a Hohmann transfer ellipse calculated by the on-board computers.

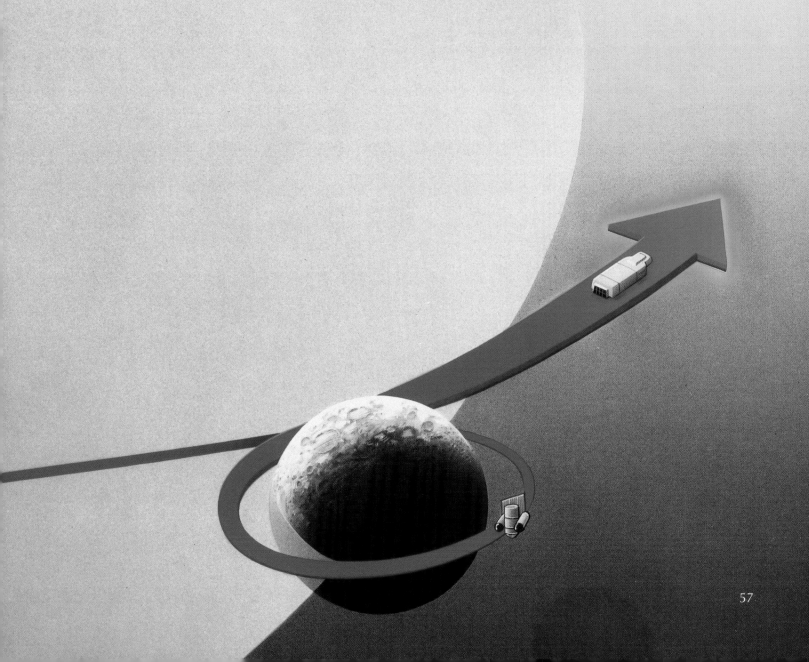

58

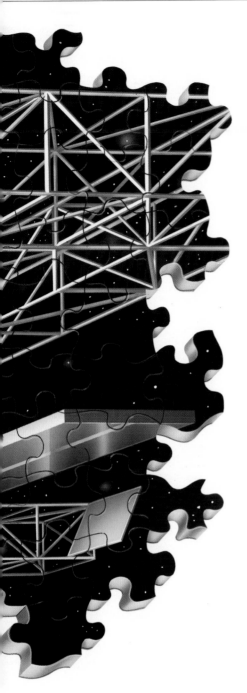

Sojourns
in Space

Even before the first manned Apollo mission lifted off, NASA had started work on an orbiting laboratory designed to be linked to Earth by the same ferry that would carry astronauts to and from the moon—the Apollo command module. Ultimately known as Skylab, the project had mission goals that related as much to the exploitation of space as to its exploration. In the orbiting vessel, astronaut-scientists were to make both terrestrial and astronomical observations, determine the biological effects of living in space, and conduct scientific and manufacturing experiments in an environment of zero gravity.

These would become familiar themes for NASA. In the 1980s, reusable shuttle craft were assigned many of the same aims, and plans call for such activities to be performed aboard a permanent space station in the 1990s. But Skylab was a thoroughly worthy pioneer of this workshop approach to space. It was, indeed, a frontiering triumph, not least in the way it used computers.

Even on Earth, Skylab was impressive. Housed in a modified Saturn IV-B rocket, the laboratory was a fully equipped research facility that encompassed more than 10,000 cubic feet. Work areas and living quarters were arranged in two cylindrical stories. At one end, beyond an air-lock module that would allow the ferry spacecraft to dock, was the Apollo telescope mount, a 12-ton observatory that held instruments for making detailed studies of the sun. Not only would the sun be an object of study, it would also be the source of power for Skylab's housekeeping and scientific operations. Once in orbit 270 miles above Earth, the lab would deploy an array of solar panels: Two large panels at the sides would form solar wings; four smaller panels would unfold atop the telescope mount like the petals of a flower.

About 10 percent of the electricity generated by the panels was earmarked for Skylab's pathbreaking computerized system—the APCS, or attitude and pointing control system, responsible primarily for governing the craft's attitude, or position along three axes relative to Earth. The APCS represented NASA's first opportunity to employ a full-function, dual-redundant computer system aboard a manned spacecraft. While Gemini and Apollo backed up the command spacecraft's on-board computer system with ground-based computers in Houston and hand-calculated solutions by the astronauts themselves, Skylab's APCS included two identical on-board computers. One functioned as the prime unit, the second as a backup; each machine was capable of performing all the necessary functions. If the system's redundancy-management software detected deviations from the craft's prescribed orientation in space, it could automatically order the prime computer to cede control to the backup. Such a switchover could also be executed by the crew or by ground control. So critical was precise attitude control to the accuracy of the mission's solar observations that the computer for the system was called the Apollo telescope-mount digital computer (ATMDC).

Unlike the special computers devised for the cramped quarters aboard Gemini and Apollo, the ATMDC had not been custom-built for Skylab. The central

59

processing unit (CPU) in each computer was from IBM's 4Pi series of processors, direct descendants of the System/360 computers developed by IBM in the early 1960s. The 4Pi model chosen for Skylab was the TC-1. It was adapted for the mission by the addition of an input/output assembly — the workshop-computer interface unit — that allowed the TC-1 to communicate with the lab's sun sensors and other instruments, as well as with various gyroscopes and control thrusters.

The use of tested, off-the-shelf technology proved so successful with Skylab that it became a standard NASA requirement for subsequent programs. But in other respects, the choice was somewhat problematic. As had been the case with the Apollo project, hardware decisions were made first, before the software specifications had been determined. For Skylab, the hardware choices were frozen by October 1969; the document spelling out program requirements was not issued until the following July. In trying to meet the program specifications, IBM produced software that ranged from 9,000 to nearly 20,000 words — but the capacity of core memory in the computers selected for the mission was only 16,000 words. As a result, IBM engineers had to request numerous alterations to NASA's program specs in order to reconfigure the software to fit without losing critical functions. Despite these obstacles, IBM delivered the final release of the software on March 20, 1973, two months before the scheduled launch.

As a further guarantee of reliability, an auxiliary system called the memory load unit (MLU) was added in mid-1971 to provide a backup. Should the software be inadvertently erased from core memory, the entire package — or an 8,000-word skeleton version — could be reloaded from a read-only tape.

SKYLAB, CELESTIAL INVALID

This fail-safe computer system faced stiff challenges at both the beginning and the end of Skylab's time in orbit. The first thing went wrong just 63 seconds after a Saturn V booster launched the workshop into the sky above Kennedy Space Center on May 14, 1973. At 28,000 feet, atmospheric drag ripped the aluminum thermal shield from the skin of the workshop. As the shield tore away, it pulled one of the solar wings half open and jammed the other wing shut. Moments later, a rocket blast flung the prematurely opened wing into space. The crippled lab made it into orbit, but without its protective shield it began to broil in the sun. Temperatures inside the workshop quickly approached 165° F., too hot for habitation by the three astronauts scheduled to take off and dock with Skylab the next day. The heat already threatened the lab's supply of medicines, food, film and sensitive equipment, and mission controllers feared it might act on the workshop's insulation to produce a deadly gas. Even if the heat were not a problem, Skylab would lack the means to power its workshop systems unless it could deploy its remaining solar wing. The quartet of solar panels on the telescope mount had unfolded according to plan when the craft reached orbit, but they were far too small to supply the current needed for all workshop functions.

Ground controllers at the Johnson Space Center in Houston and engineers at the Marshall Space Flight Center in Huntsville, Alabama, reckoned it would take days — perhaps weeks — to devise emergency repairs that an astronaut team could carry out. But Skylab's systems needed immediate infusions of solar energy: Without them, the $2.6-billion program would be reduced to an orbiting scrap heap. NASA hurriedly scrubbed the next day's launch, then ordered contractors and its own engineers to find ways to cool the craft and free its solar wing. Luckily, the engineers had help, at least with the heating problem. In contrast to Skylab's external injuries, the on-board computer system was functioning flawlessly. While others cobbled up long-range repair plans and makeshift sun shields, William Chubb and the Skylab team for attitude control enlisted the APCS in the task of reconciling two conflicting requirements: The four small solar panels had to be positioned to receive maximum sun exposure to generate electricity for the ailing ship, but at the same time, the unshielded workshop itself had to be rotated to protect its equipment from excessive sun.

Fortunately, the computer system had been designed to accommodate direct commands from the ground. For 11 days straight, working in round-the-clock shifts, Chubb's staff fed a constant stream of new orders via radio telemetry into Skylab's prime computer through a receiver on the air-lock module. The labor paid off, but Steve Bales, a veteran Apollo controller, later remembered that period as "the hardest two weeks I have ever spent."

Even as the attitude control team pulled emergency duty to keep Skylab appropriately aligned until the astronauts could make physical repairs, some of the team's members were working on more permanent fixes. Over the next few weeks, the team devised more than a dozen patches, delivered via radio telemetry, to overwrite the relevant portions of the program stored in the on-board computer's core memory. Chubb and his colleagues had actually identified a few of the patches before the launch, as part of a first-aid kit of 24 software solutions to potential flight problems. But the rest had to be fashioned in the high-pressure atmosphere of imminent disaster, a challenge that drew on the collective efforts of five separate programming teams. The reprogramming was vital to the lab's ultimate survival, but as Chubb recalled many years later, "If we hadn't had the ability to monitor and correct Skylab's attitude by issuing commands to the on-board computer, we wouldn't have been able to make the mission at all."

At last, on May 25, astronauts Charles Conrad Jr., Joseph P. Kerwin and Paul J. Weitz — armed with an assortment of improvised tools and a "we can fix anything" attitude — blasted off for their belated rendezvous with the orbiting lab. At the end of a seven-and-a-half-hour chase, Conrad and his crew caught up with their target and succeeded in docking. Following a night in the cramped quarters of the Apollo craft, the astronauts entered the lab, cautiously testing for toxic gas as they went. None was detected: The quick work by the attitude control team had prevented any damage to the insulation. Now the space crew's first task was to rig a giant parasol to compensate for the missing heat shield. Using an extensible pole, Conrad and Weitz thrust the collapsible rectangular umbrella from inside the workshop out through a small air lock and opened it to shade the lab's exposed side. Immediately, the workshop's skin temperature dropped by as much as 60 degrees. By their fifth night in space, as the temperature in the workshop dropped to a bearable 80° F., the crew moved into their living quarters for the first time.

The jammed solar wing was a more recalcitrant problem. On June 7, nearly two weeks after their arrival in orbit, Conrad and Kerwin put on their spacesuits and ventured outside with modified pruning shears mounted on the end of a long pole. It took the pair four hours of awkward, weightless struggle to sever the aluminum strap that pinioned the wing. But when the panel at last swung free, power flowed through its solar cells and into the workshop systems. The word radioed from Mission Control was jubilant: "We see amps!"

Skylab was a working laboratory again. The first crew spent a total of 28 days aloft, returning to Earth on June 22. Just before the crew left, Mission Control put their key fail-safe theory to the test: On a signal from the ground, operational control switched over from the prime ATMDC to the backup. The switch took place uneventfully, and for the remainder of the lab's 272-day mission, the erstwhile backup was in control. Two more crews occupied Skylab over the next eight months, for 59 and 84 days respectively. Throughout Skylab's working life, the battered lab surpassed all NASA's hopes, as its crews collected volumes of invaluable data — tracking the comet Kohoutek, surveying Earth, photographing solar flares and monitoring their own physical reactions to living in space. On February 8, 1974, the crew of *Skylab 3* splash-landed in the Pacific, having traveled 34.5 million miles and broken the existing records for time in space, distance traveled and number of space walks.

The day after splashdown, ground controllers vented Skylab's atmosphere and maneuvered the craft into its storage attitude: docking adapter pointed spaceward and solar panels trailing. The ground crew then deactivated all of Skylab's systems except the air-lock module command receiver. But before leaving the laboratory to hibernate in space, the staff at Mission Control tried an experiment. Curious whether the on-board memory load unit would still function, they signaled the MLU to load the taped backup program into memory. This accomplished, the ground crew paused to verify that the program was running properly and then indulged in a final display of long-distance control: successfully reloading the entire 16,000-word package from the ground. This exercise — the first time an in-flight computer had been fully loaded by a radio-frequency uplink — proved to be a dress rehearsal for events that would take place nearly half a decade later.

PLANS GONE AWRY

NASA knew that Skylab's orbit would gradually decay over the next several years, causing the workshop to plummet to Earth unless a rescue mission could reach it in time. Calculations made in 1974 suggested that Skylab would remain aloft until March 1983, by which time NASA planned to have a new project up and running: The Space Transportation System, or space shuttle, as it was better known, was due to launch in the late 1970s. Shuttle astronauts would thus be on hand to boost Skylab into a higher orbit by attaching a propulsion module to the workshop. Failing that — or some other solution — Skylab would disintegrate as it reentered Earth's atmosphere, showering debris onto the surface below.

Nine years seemed ample time to decide what to do about the 100-ton hulk before it reappeared in the form of metal rain. In 1977, however, unusually intense solar activity increased the density of the atmosphere at Skylab's orbital altitude, markedly increasing the drag on the spacecraft. By that autumn, Skylab was tumbling like a runaway beer barrel, losing altitude much faster than expected. Predictions for its reentry suddenly shifted to early 1979, even 1978, and NASA scrambled to find a way to prolong the workshop's orbital life.

Whatever could be done, if anything, would depend on the condition of Skylab's on-board computer system and on the ability of NASA's engineers to

communicate with a spacecraft in suspended animation. On March 6, 1978, a team of engineers at NASA's ground station in Bermuda beamed a radio signal at Skylab, hoping to converse with the craft through its telemetry system. But Skylab's batteries had long since run down, and the craft was spinning so rapidly that its power-giving solar panels were only intermittently exposed to the sun.

"We knew we'd only have it for that little window of time," William Chubb said later. "We tried and tried to talk to its telemetry, and finally it talked back to us. That was a very emotional moment for all of us." For two brief minutes, Skylab reported on its condition; then, as the tumbling craft turned its solar panels into shadow, the transmissions ceased.

Clearly the team's priority was to recharge Skylab's batteries. This required nearly a week of orbital passes through fleeting periods of sunlight. Next, the NASA engineers had to ascertain whether the ATMDC was functional and then try to enlist the computer's help in stabilizing the spacecraft. The engineers worried that the hardware or software — or both — might have gone bad since last used. On March 11, the NASA team signaled Skylab's system, hoping to obtain telemetry confirmation that the ATMDC was still capable of a degree of control. It was. Resuming the program cycle precisely where it had left off four years and 30 days earlier, the system functioned for a full five minutes. "It was as if it had never stopped," Chubb said later.

Now it was up to the reentry team to prompt Skylab's computer to begin salvage operations. To this end, the team devised two new control systems. The first, called end-on-velocity vector, or EOVV, was designed to wrench the craft out of its high-drag sideways orientation and point its tapered end in the direction of flight. The second system, called torque equilibrium attitude, would be activated only if Skylab began plunging earthward; the new program was intended to steady the space lab as it fell, then tumble it at a critical moment during reentry so that it would come down over water.

With the reprogramming completed, Skylab's movements were once again governed exclusively by computer. NASA's engineers could do little more than hope that the craft would stay aloft long enough to allow a shuttle mission to push it higher. If Skylab did fall, the engineers were praying, the new last-minute, computer-controlled tumbling maneuver would keep the metal bits and pieces from landing on anything — or anyone — that might get hurt.

Under the guidance of the reactivated on-board system, the lab pursued its course for more than a year. But near the end of that time, Skylab's orbit was eroding too fast for the craft to wait for a salvage shuttle that was still more than a year away from getting off the ground. Early in July 1979, NASA predicted that the workshop would reenter the atmosphere on July 11, breaking up as it approached the east coast of the United States and ultimately cascading into open ocean near Australia. A newspaper in San Francisco offered $10,000 to the first person delivering an authentic piece of the wreckage within 48 hours of impact.

But Skylab, true to its unpredictable beginnings, refused to follow the script. The lab did not break up when it was supposed to; instead, it stayed intact until it had gone past the United States and Africa, then splintered apart and rained down on farmland southeast of Perth, Australia. Luckily, the space-age precipitation injured no one, and for 17-year-old truck driver Stan Thornton, the saga of America's first space station came to an unexpectedly lucrative close. Discovering some charred fragments in his backyard in the seaside town of Esperance, Thornton sped with them to the airport and caught the first plane for California. There the pieces were identified as fragments of Skylab's insulation, and Thornton returned to Australia $10,000 richer.

A CALCULATING CRAFT

For most of Skylab's time in orbit, the on-board computer had served as much more than the fourth crew member, as the astronauts called it: It was the only crew member. And in many ways, the system set the stage for a major expansion of the computer's role in manned space flight. Building on Skylab's foundation of redundancy-management software and dual computers, the space shuttle would be the most automated craft in history.

Touted as a reusable successor to the disposable spacecraft of all previous programs, the shuttle was a product of NASA's straitened circumstances in the early 1970s, when much of the agency's money was siphoned off to finance social programs and the Vietnam War. If the space program was to evolve from one-shot extravaganzas to a pay-as-you-go feasibility, it required a vehicle that would not need to be met by small fleets of recovery ships and aircraft at the end of a mission. The shuttle was designed to fly as many as 100 missions before having to be grounded for overhaul. More significant, its flight deck and cargo bay would be leased to commercial ventures, other federal agencies, and even foreign governments to haul people and a variety of payloads into orbit. In 1972, NASA administrator James Fletcher called the shuttle "the only meaningful new manned space program that can be accomplished on a modest budget."

However modest the shuttle's budget, the role of its on-board computers was the most ambitious yet. The shuttle literally could not fly without them. In conventional aircraft, the pilot manipulates a joystick and foot pedals to control the movement of aerodynamic surfaces through mechanical and hydraulic linkages. As the surfaces respond, the pilot adjusts the controls accordingly, and the cycle begins again. In the shuttle, computers come between the pilot and the control surfaces in this feedback loop, most of the time replacing the pilot altogether: Sensors at various points on the craft relay information — attitude and velocity, for example — along electrical wires to the craft's computers. The computers then issue programmed commands, also in the form of electrical signals, to hydraulic actuators at the control surfaces. As the actuators respond, the sensors send new information back to the computers. In addition to flight control, the shuttle's computers also handle navigation and guidance and such system-management functions as the monitoring of fuel levels and life-support systems, once the province of human beings at Mission Control.

A DIVISION OF LABOR
Having lived through the Apollo software war, NASA knew the scope of the development task that lay ahead and was determined to maintain tight supervision of the process. Thus, although the contract for shuttle assembly went to Rockwell International, the job of producing the spacecraft's software fell to IBM, in a separate contract that spelled out the software requirements.

Rockwell was taken aback at first when it realized it was not being given all parts of the shuttle job. But since the company had been planning to subcontract all the computer work to IBM in any case, they followed through and handed off the hardware portion. The processor IBM settled on was the 4Pi AP-101, the top of the line of the 4Pi series; used in aircraft since the late 1960s, the general-purpose 4Pi architecture was familiar to many programmers. As in the Skylab system, each AP-101 was coupled with a custom-built input/output processor that enabled the CPU to communicate with sensors, flight controls, guidance platforms and various other instruments in the shuttle's 38 subsystems.

Because the shuttle was such a complex anomaly — it had to maneuver in orbit like a spacecraft, yet be capable of aerodynamic flight on reentering Earth's atmosphere to land on solid ground — the on-board computers would need to govern every aspect of the mission. IBM's system had to be utterly reliable. That ideal was achieved through full redundancy, an advancement of the dual system used on Skylab. On the shuttle, four identical AP-101s functioned simultaneously in a quadruple-redundant set during critical flight phases such as ascent and reentry, processing the same information in precise synchronization *(pages 80-81)*. If a conflict arose among the four, the majority ruled, voting the conflicting unit out of the loop. None of the computers, singly or en masse, could turn off any other: That step was left to the crew. An errant machine announced itself by warning lights, audio signals and display-screen messages suggesting that the crew might want to pull the plug.

To guard against the possibility of a bug in the primary software — an error that would be duplicated in all primary computers and therefore would be undetectable and uncorrectable — a fifth AP-101 served as a fail-safe backup. Its software had fewer functions, but it could nonetheless safely accomplish a no-frills ascent or reentry in case the quadruple-redundant set failed. Software for the backup computer was written not by IBM but by Rockwell to minimize the likelihood of a common error. Reliability projections showed that the possibility of failure in the computer quartet was so remote it would cause only four aircraft losses in a thousand million flights. Furthermore, redundancy not only made shuttle missions safer, it also lightened their demands on ground control. "With the shuttle," said one member of Houston's ground crew, "we are talking about four controllers manning a flight, versus hundreds on a full-blown Apollo mission."

FLUENCY IN A NEW LANGUAGE

With the principle of redundancy solidly established, the remaining challenge was to write the shuttle's software. The huge expense and difficulties suffered in the development of software for Apollo caused NASA to take a hard look at the language in which the shuttle's programs would be written. Much of Apollo's software had been meticulously coded in assembly language, which required the programmer to pay attention to the computer's machine-instruction set and to sequences of addresses in memory. To give programmers greater flexibility, NASA urged the creation of a new computer language for the shuttle project. Similar in concept to Project Apollo's ATOLL, the language would allow programmers to focus on solving the problem at hand — in this case, devising a flight control system for the shuttle — without getting bogged down in the mechanics of translating program instructions into language the computer can understand.

The language selected was HAL/S, created especially for the shuttle by Intermetrics, Inc., a Massachusetts company founded in 1969 by five M.I.T. programmers who had worked on developing software for Apollo. The language's name was a tribute to computer pioneer J. Halcombe Laning, who in 1952 invented an algebraic compiler to run on M.I.T.'s Whirlwind, the first computer capable of operating in real time. Laning also collaborated on an early language called MAC, which contributed heavily to HAL/S. Ed Copps, one of Intermetrics' founders, won a bottle of Scotch for coining the name HAL in a company-sponsored contest. The *S*, standing simply for "subset," won no awards.

What set HAL/S apart from other computer languages available in the 1970s was its ability to schedule tasks according to priority levels defined by the programmer. Distilled from the best existing programming techniques, HAL/S defined strict access rules that allowed the segments of a program to interact only as the program's author intended. But the language's greatest distinction may have been that it featured specific statements for real-time computing: Several programs appeared to share computer processing simultaneously, allowing both the crew and the many automatic systems controlled by the computer to respond to rapidly changing events inside and outside the spacecraft.

Waiting on the launch pad at Kennedy Space Center on the morning of April 10, 1981, the shuttle was the beneficiary of a decade of intensive computer engineering. But all that effort was invisible. From the outside, the shuttle resembled nothing so much as a crude skyscraper: The tallest tower, a 154-foot-high tank, contained liquid propellant for the orbiter's three main engines. Buttressing the main tank were two reusable rocket boosters, containing the first solid fuel to propel a manned NASA spacecraft. Riding piggyback on the main tank was the delta-winged orbiter, *Columbia,* the airplane-like component that carried not only the payload but — thanks to the reliability of its computers — a human crew on this, its maiden flight. Aboard *Columbia* were mission commander John Young and pilot Robert Crippen. At 50, Young was a space veteran — his first venture had been as the pilot aboard *Gemini 3* in 1965, and he had walked on the moon during the mission of *Apollo 16.* Crippen, 43, had been waiting a dozen years for his first space flight; he had been selected for the shuttle's inaugural voyage because of his familiarity with its data-processing system.

The computer crew included the five general-purpose AP-101 computers as well as a host of more-specialized supporting players. A pair of dedicated computers controlled each of the three main engines, for example. Other processors tended to such mundane chores as managing data-bus traffic, ushering programs in and out of mass memory, and displaying information on the three screens in the cockpit. The information the astronauts read there would almost entirely supplant communications from ground control.

But 20 minutes before *Columbia's* scheduled lift-off that April morning, the backup computer signaled that something was wrong. "It made my console light up like a Christmas tree," said a Houston controller. The countdown came to a halt — and eventually the launch was scrubbed — while engineers and flight controllers tried to track down the malfunction.

By early afternoon, NASA's troubleshooters had isolated the problem. It was a timing skew, a minuscule programming error that had survived thousands of hours of testing. Because of it, all four primary computers had begun functioning 40 milliseconds earlier than they should have. Since the backup computer always eavesdropped on the others to gain up-to-the-second information should it have to take over, its attempt to synchronize with the primary flight software at T-minus-20 resulted in a rebuff. Interpreting the timing disparity to mean that it was out of step, the backup computer promptly "hung up the phone," in the words of one engineer.

The problem stemmed in part from a difference in philosophy between the operating systems written by Rockwell and by IBM. The Rockwell-authored backup software was time-sliced, or synchronous, meaning it dedicated a specific slice of time to each processing task and executed those tasks in a fixed order. In contrast, IBM's software for the primary computers was priority-interrupt-driven, or asynchronous; it performed computations on demand and in strict observance of their predefined importance.

Rockwell and IBM had disagreed over the comparative merits of each system for two years. They need not have. NASA engineers determined that the bug would appear only once in 67 launches, so they restarted the computers, and *Columbia* was ready to go again in less than 48 hours. Whatever its origins, the problem had never disrupted the smooth functioning of the primary software. It would not have kept the backup software from running either, had the backup

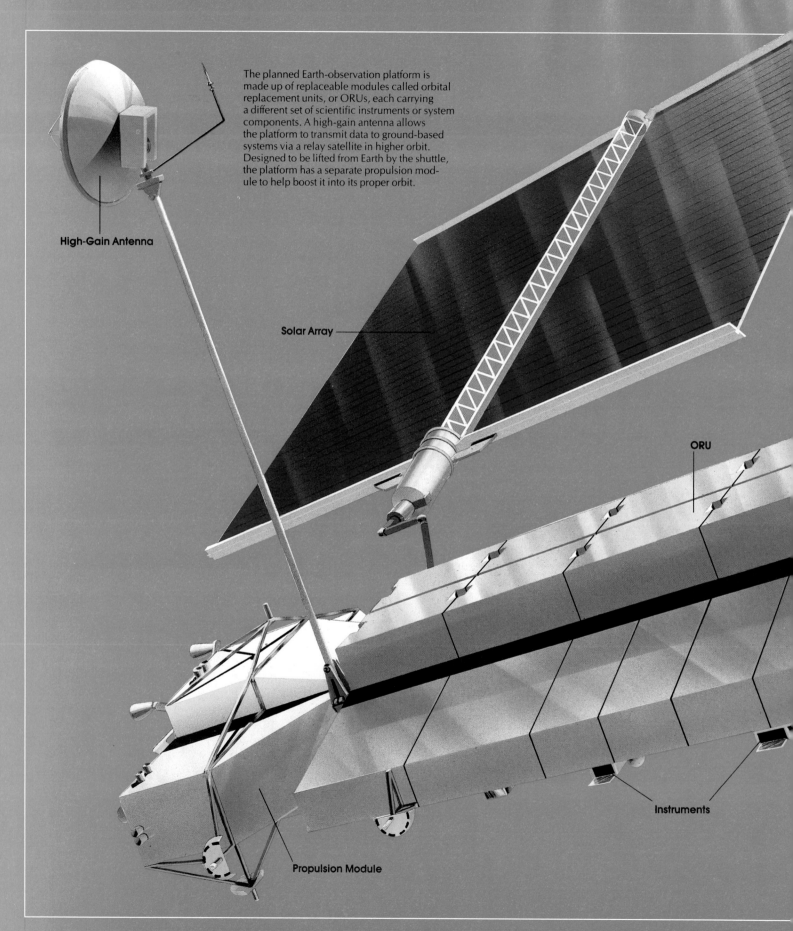

The planned Earth-observation platform is
made up of replaceable modules called orbital
replacement units, or ORUs, each carrying
a different set of scientific instruments or system
components. A high-gain antenna allows
the platform to transmit data to ground-based
systems via a relay satellite in higher orbit.
Designed to be lifted from Earth by the shuttle,
the platform has a separate propulsion module to help boost it into its proper orbit.

High-Gain Antenna

Solar Array

ORU

Instruments

Propulsion Module

A Multi-Purpose Observer in Orbit

NASA's plans for space stations in low Earth orbit call not only for a manned structure where astronauts and scientists can carry out experiments and observations but also a variety of unmanned structures. Coorbiting platforms, for example — platforms whose orbital plane usually makes the same angle with the equator as that of the manned station — will serve as astrophysics observatories or as zero-gravity laboratories for processing delicate materials.

The Earth-observation platform illustrated here is intended to circle the globe in a north-south polar orbit at an altitude of 512 miles. Carried into orbit by the space shuttle, the platform will be repaired and serviced by astronauts, either on extravehicular duty or using the remote manipulators. The modular design of the platform will give scientists the opportunity to reconfigure its array of instruments as the mission progresses.

The goal of the Earth-observing mission is to provide scientists with a source of comprehensive information. By flying a number of sensors on a single structure, in an orbit that permits the system to map Earth once every one or two days, scientists can merge data not easily correlated from separate satellites with different viewing times and mapping cycles. Together with ground-based studies, long-term data collected from such a mission will help scientists to establish trends in the world's climate, for example, or to understand the workings of the oceans (below).

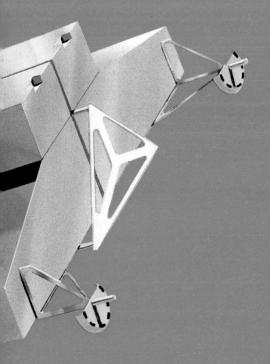

These computer-generated images (right), based on data collected by an experimental NASA satellite in polar orbit, reveal changes in the distribution of microscopic plants called phytoplankton in the ocean off the west coast of South America. In one year, phytoplankton concentration in offshore waters went from very low (top, dark blue) to high and widespread (bottom, orange). Scientists hope that the comprehensive data provided by a space platform will give them a better understanding of the timing and scale of oceanographic processes that have an effect on the growth and distribution of these tiny plants, which are the first link in the oceanic food chain.

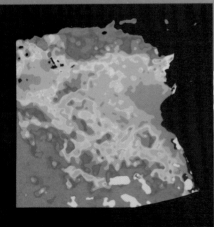

only been allowed to join in. Moreover, during subsequent shuttle missions, both systems ran without fault.

At 7 a.m. on April 12, 1981 — nearly six years since NASA's last manned flight and 20 years to the day since Soviet cosmonaut Yuri Gagarin became the first human in space — *Columbia* rose into the sky with a blast that flattened several hundred feet of wire fence and shook buildings miles away. Once under way, the voyage went just as everyone had hoped it would: routinely. Young and Crippen had no trouble putting the craft through its computerized paces. But despite exhaustive planning and testing, the shuttle software could not be completely immunized from error; from time to time on succeeding missions, glitches popped up. Given that possibility, shuttle astronauts were required to carry around a manual called *Program Notes and Waivers*. The notes detailed software idiosyncracies the user might find hard to fathom; the waivers described unworkable anomalies — bugs, that is. Depending on the mission, the manual often ran to 200 pages.

ALTERING A SATELLITE'S STATE
Despite these drawbacks, spaceborne computers, both on and off the shuttle, were known to come through in a pinch. In February 1980, NASA launched the Solar Maximum Mission satellite — Solar Max for short — to study solar flares during the climax in the sun's 11-year sunspot cycle. After 10 months of flawless performance, three fuses blew out in the satellite's attitude-control box, leaving Solar Max unable to hold its proper orientation in space and disabling most of its instruments. Engineers at the Goddard Space Flight Center, the satellite's tracking facility in Greenbelt, Maryland, managed to keep Solar Max from shutting down entirely by switching to its backup attitude-control system. They placed it in an orderly conning spin, its solar panels pointing toward the sun, and left it to drift for three years until a shuttle mission could be sent to its rescue.

On the rendezvous morning of April 8, 1984, mission specialist George Nelson used a free-flying jet-propelled backpack to traverse the 100 feet to Solar Max from the shuttle *Challenger*. Nelson hoped to steady the satellite and hold it motionless long enough for the shuttle's manipulator arm to scoop it into the cargo bay. But Nelson's grappling device refused to clamp onto Solar Max, and each attempt to dock with the satellite jostled it into an increasingly erratic tumble. The solar panels lost contact with the sun, and power began to ebb from the batteries. New tactics were needed — and quickly.

In a replay of the kind of effort that gained control of Skylab in its last days, Goddard's engineers temporarily took over. Using long-range telemetry command, they overwrote the attitude-control program in the satellite's computer memory with a program that employed a different position-sensing method. Solar Max began to right itself almost instantly. Soon it was nearly still, and its solar panels began recharging the batteries. The next day, ground-based engineers reloaded the original attitude-control program into Solar Max's computers. *Challenger* sidled up to the now-docile satellite, and the astronauts plucked it from space with the manipulator arm. Working in the cargo hold, two spacesuited astronauts repaired the satellite in about an hour and 45 minutes. Returned to orbit, Solar Max resumed its work at once.

More than just salvaging an invaluable observatory, the rescue of Solar Max proved that astronauts and computers could collaborate successfully and demonstrated the shuttle's ability to make money-saving service calls in space. Both achievements foreshadowed much of what is expected from a manned space station in permanent orbit around Earth.

FROM SPACE RACE TO SPACE BASE

Fiction writers have been fabricating inhabited stations in space for a long time. One of the earliest to do so was Boston clergyman Edward Everett Hale, who in 1869 envisioned a large, hollow sphere, built of ordinary house bricks and hurled into the heavens by a gigantic waterfall-driven flywheel. Since then, whimsy has given way to a more probable concept: The space station on NASA's drawing boards for the 1990s is intended to be both a zero-gravity research facility in near-Earth orbit and a springboard for future missions to deep space.

By the mid-1980s, much of the practical research needed to make the space station a reality had already been done. Both the transportation system and the tools to put the station together had been checked out. For instance, during a mission in November 1985 to practice space-station assembly, a pair of astronauts from the shuttle *Atlantis* worked outside their craft to fit together two types of cumbersome aluminum structures. On Earth, the parts would have weighed several hundred pounds — impossible for two humans to manipulate unaided.

Like the rest of NASA's programs, the space station suffered a severe setback in the aftermath of the shuttle *Challenger* disaster, the worst shock in the history of the American space program. Seventy-six seconds after launch on January 28, 1986, a devastating explosion ignited by a leak in a solid-fuel rocket booster destroyed *Challenger* and its seven crew members. The irony, and the pity, was that for all the computerization and redundancy built into the shuttle's systems, the rocket boosters, once ignited, were one element over which the computers had absolutely no control.

NASA and the rest of the space industry spent many months reevaluating their methods, systems and priorities, particularly with regard to future missions. Although the shuttle may no longer carry commercial payloads, NASA still plans to use the transport system in the construction of the space station. According to these plans, shuttle flights will haul aloft prefabricated aluminum modules, then park them in orbit 250 miles high for assembly. Ultimately, using the shuttle's robot arm and other tools and cranes tailored to the task, shuttle crews will maneuver the floating modules into place and yoke them securely together.

Computers will then play a critical role in the operation and maintenance of the completed station. Indeed, automation of one sort or another will characterize almost every aspect of the station, to a degree that should surpass even the highly computerized space shuttle.

Perhaps the most visionary plans for the space station — and certainly the ones that will require the most memory capacity — are those involving the application of artificial intelligence, or AI. The space base of the early 21st century might be managed almost entirely by so-called expert systems, programs that combine logical reasoning and problem-solving techniques with a store of experience and data mined from human experts. Linked in an interactive network, a number of such systems might operate in concert, making individual decisions and informing one another of the results. High on the agenda of this computerized managerial committee will be housekeeping functions: Expert systems will be charged with supervising the astronauts' environmental control and life-support systems, as well as directing space-station subsystems for electrical power, propulsion, communication and tracking. With AI advances in the field of robot vision and mobility, computerized workers might be employed both in the assembly of the space station and in its servicing and maintenance. By taking over chores within the station and in the vacuum of space, robots would free the human crew to concentrate on celestial observation and scientific experiments.

Ultimately, artificial intelligence programs might be combined to create an additional automated astronaut, rounding out the standard crew of eight. As conceived by Frederick J. Dickey of Boeing's Artificial Intelligence Center in Bellevue, Washington, the crew's electronic colleague would be "a disembodied intelligence" at the command of the space station's computer system. The automated astronaut might take any number of incarnations. In its capacity as an expert system, it could keep the space base up and running, an activity that would otherwise occupy two human crew members. Alternatively, the extra astronaut could command a robot to act as surrogate labor in such hazardous tasks as extravehicular repairs and servicing. Autonomy for those operations would come in increments. At first, humans would monitor the on-board automated systems, granting them a growing measure of independence only as their performance warranted.

Without doubt, the challenge of creating space-station software will make even the programming headaches of Apollo, Skylab and the space shuttle pale by comparison. For all its promise, artificial intelligence research is still in its childhood at best; much work remains to be done before the automated astronaut will be able to learn from experience, a critical element in making sound decisions in emergencies. Even the development of such human-like senses as vision and touch requires highly complex — and as yet unperfected — programming.

But assuming the space station is fully functional in low-Earth orbit by the year 2000 — with or without an autonomous electronic crew member — one scenario proposed by the National Commission on Space foresees a transport system to hopscotch cargoes and passengers from base to base and thence to outer worlds. The space station would eventually become merely a point of departure for human settlements on the moon or Mars, or for a string of ports and colonies reaching ever deeper into space.

That schedule for colonizing the cosmos represents one small step toward corroborating a prediction made early on by rocket engineer Wernher von Braun. Even as rookie human crews were beginning to learn the ropes of space travel, von Braun foresaw the 21st century as "the century of scientific and commercial activity in outer space, of manned interplanetary flights and the beginnings of the establishment of permanent human footholds outside the mother planet Earth." Although von Braun omitted mention of automated systems, they have actually gone before, in the guise of robot probes that have spent the past decade exploring the solar system. Humanity will seek to follow the trail computers have already blazed.

A Battery of Backups

No human or team of humans could pilot the United States' space shuttle into orbit aided only by the five senses. The craft has too much power and goes too fast. Human reaction times are far too slow.

What makes shuttle flight possible is an elaborate computer system built into the vehicle. In the ascent to orbit, a critical stage of a mission, the computers run the show, and during all phases of a mission they serve as intermediaries in a flight-control system called "flying by wire." In this arrangement, mechanical links — between throttle and engine, for example — are replaced by computer links that receive signals from flight-deck controls and convert them into commands for the shuttle's machinery.

The shuttle is utterly dependent on its electronic aids. A complete failure of the shuttle's computers during ascent or reentry would transform the spacecraft into an inert, uncontrollable object. Consequently, the computer system must be extraordinarily reliable. To make it so, NASA selected the IBM AP-101 computer, the latest of a flight-proven family of machines used for weapon systems control in B-52 bombers and other combat aircraft, to serve as the shuttle's general-purpose computer (GPC).

But even the best computer can occasionally go on the blink, as NASA had learned from earlier projects. To compensate for this frailty, the shuttle has several GPCs. As many as four of them continuously run identical software, simultaneously and independently, in a system of checks and balances that reduces the possibility of error. If one computer in this quadruple-redundant set-up weighs in with a calculation that differs from results produced by the other computers, the majority rules. Tie votes alert the crew that it may be necessary to switch to yet another GPC, a backup computer running different software. The backup would allow a safe emergency landing if the other GPCs were all somehow disabled.

While computers make shuttle flight feasible, they do not make it easy. To communicate with the computers during a 58-hour shuttle flight, the crew might perform 13,000 keystrokes, the same number required for an Apollo mission to the moon that lasted three times as long. So much attention do the computers require that it seemed to John Young, chief astronaut in the early 1980s, that crew members "end up working for the computers, rather than the computers working for us."

73

Five Computers for the Work of One

In every aspect of the shuttle, from sensors to communication channels, redundancy is the shuttle's secret for reliability. No system aboard the shuttle profits more from redundancy than the computer system. Although a single one of the craft's general-purpose computers (GPCs) can run an entire shuttle mission, there are six of the machines aboard, one of them unconnected.

The degree of computer redundancy varies as a flight unfolds. Quadruple redundancy applies during ascent and descent, when computer failure could result in the loss of shuttle and crew. Four GPCs all run the shuttle's primary avionics software system (PASS), an intricate program tailored to each shuttle flight by a team of IBM programmers. The fifth GPC runs the backup flight system (BFS), written independently by Rockwell International programmers. The astronauts would call on the backup computer to operate the shuttle if an error in the PASS were to disable the other four GPC.

In orbit, two GPCs steer the shuttle while one helps to control the manipulator arm and monitor various systems aboard the orbiter. The other two—one loaded with an extra copy of the reentry software, the other with the BFS—are turned off to conserve power.

During ascent, four redundant gyroscope units in the rear of the shuttle monitor changes in the spacecraft's attitude and then forward identical reports to the GPCs on the mid-deck. The computers steer the shuttle by commanding hydraulic actuators to swivel the main engines in their mountings. Once in orbit, the craft is steered by two orbital maneuvering engines and 44 small hydrazine thrusters.

Gyroscope Unit

Main-Engine Actuator

Main Engines

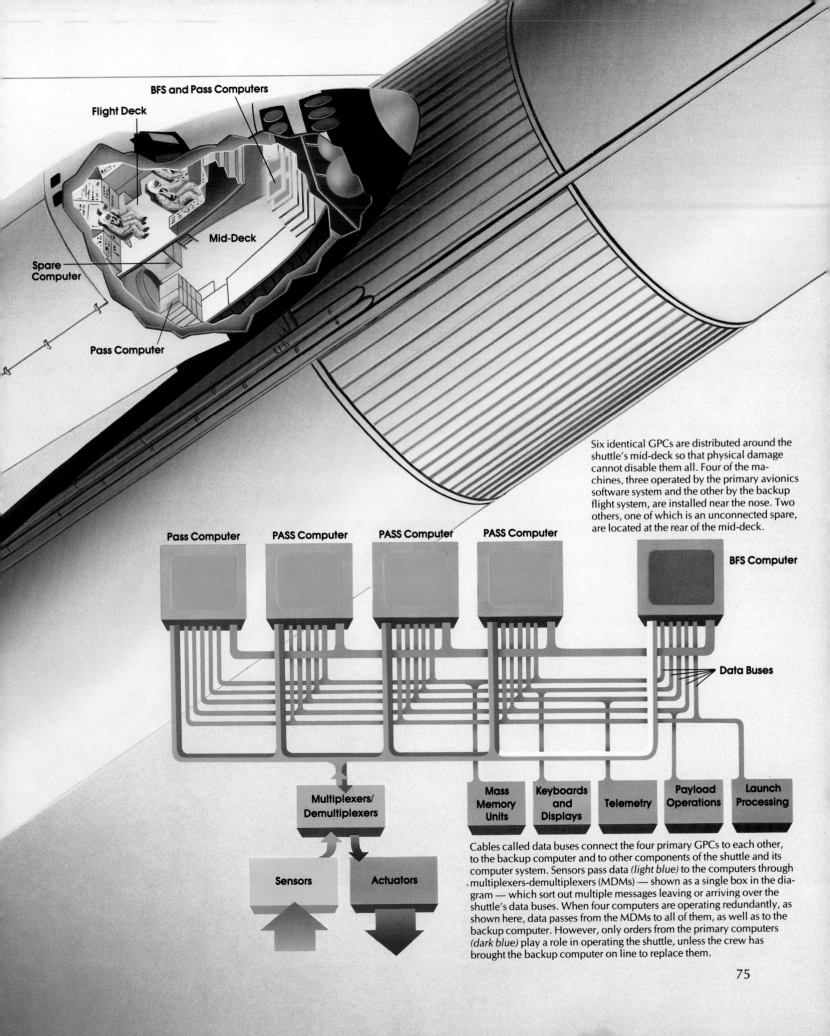

Flight Deck

BFS and Pass Computers

Mid-Deck

Spare Computer

Pass Computer

Six identical GPCs are distributed around the shuttle's mid-deck so that physical damage cannot disable them all. Four of the machines, three operated by the primary avionics software system and the other by the backup flight system, are installed near the nose. Two others, one of which is an unconnected spare, are located at the rear of the mid-deck.

Pass Computer   **PASS Computer**   **PASS Computer**   **PASS Computer**   **BFS Computer**

Data Buses

Multiplexers/ Demultiplexers

Mass Memory Units   **Keyboards and Displays**   **Telemetry**   **Payload Operations**   **Launch Processing**

Sensors   **Actuators**

Cables called data buses connect the four primary GPCs to each other, to the backup computer and to other components of the shuttle and its computer system. Sensors pass data (light blue) to the computers through multiplexers-demultiplexers (MDMs) — shown as a single box in the diagram — which sort out multiple messages leaving or arriving over the shuttle's data buses. When four computers are operating redundantly, as shown here, data passes from the MDMs to all of them, as well as to the backup computer. However, only orders from the primary computers (dark blue) play a role in operating the shuttle, unless the crew has brought the backup computer on line to replace them.

A Program Module for Each Phase of Flight

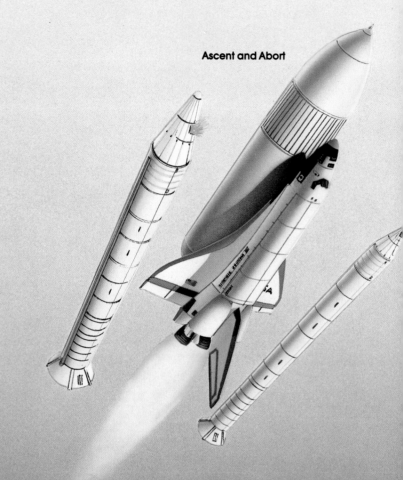

Ascent and Abort

Computer programs commonly overflow the memory available to them as unforeseen tasks and complications arise. The primary avionics software system (PASS), consisting of programs that get the shuttle into space and back, is no exception. NASA originally expected the PASS to fit into approximately 33,000 computer words of memory. But it grew to 700,000 words, far exceeding the 106,000-word memory of the on-board computers.

In order for the PASS to function within the limited memory available, programmers divided it into an operating system *(below)*, which would reside in memory during an entire mission, and seven modules, called operational sequences (OPSs), that corresponded to different stages of a flight. Because the OPSs would not all fit into the computers at the same time, those for use later in the mission had to be stored on board until they were needed. To accomplish this, NASA added something called a mass memory unit to the shuttle.

The MMU, as it is known, is essentially a tape recorder. In keeping with NASA's insistence on redundancy, the MMU contains two players, each with a 600-foot reel of half-inch tape. Each reel can store approximately 8.5 million words of software, enough capacity for three copies of the PASS — creating six layers of redundancy in all — as well as backup copies of software that governs the backup computer, the main engine controllers and the instrument-panel displays.

Preflight Initialization

Mass Memory Utility

40 MILLISECONDS	Obtain sensor data from multiplexers/demultiplexers. Send commands to multiplexers/demultiplexers. Process rate-gyro sensor data.
80 MILLISECONDS	Process attitude information and display for crew. Read pressure data from solid rocket boosters.
160 MILLISECONDS	Accept commands from Earth. Prepare and execute solid rocket booster separation. Create commands for actuators.
320 MILLISECONDS	Use input from sensors to steer vehicle into orbit. Convert sensor navigation data for display to crew.
960 MILLISECONDS	Determine vehicle location in relation to its departure point. Process data from on-board radar systems. Check rate-gyro sensors for failure.
UNSCHEDULED	Process input from crew keyboards. Execute emergency guidance functions.

This chart lists computer tasks aboard the shuttle in order of priority. At the top of the list are examples of critical jobs that the PASS operating system turns to at 40-millisecond intervals. Tasks that the computer addresses less often or only as required appear lower on the chart. To get the most important jobs done first, the computer suspends a job when one of higher priority is pending.

Orbital Check-out

Orbital Guidance, Control and Navigation

Orbital System Management

Reentry, Approach and Landing

As illustrated here, different operational sequence (OPS) programs are loaded into four of the on-board computers at each stage of a mission. When one group of OPSs has served its purpose, the next group replaces it, moving into computer memory from the mass memory unit along a data bus reserved for that purpose *(yellow)*. No OPSs are loaded into the fifth computer; it is controlled by the backup flight system, not the PASS.

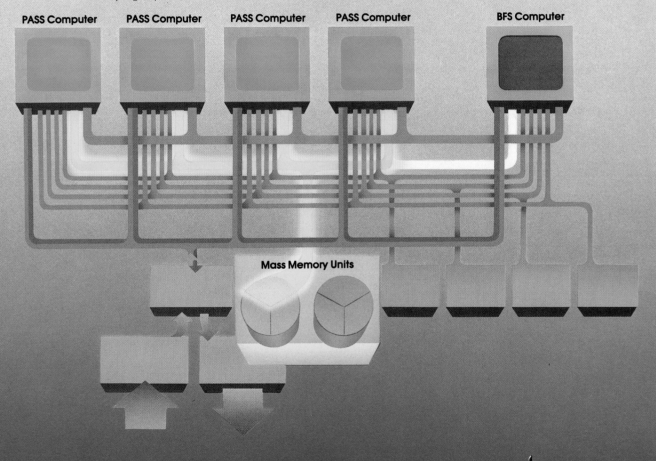

PASS Computer **PASS Computer** **PASS Computer** **PASS Computer** **BFS Computer**

Mass Memory Units

Distributing Data to the Computers

Redundancy aboard the space shuttle depends on a fine sense of timing among the four general-purpose computers operated by the primary avionics software system. As each machine taps a rapid drumbeat of calculations, it monitors the others playing at the same rhythm. Because all four computers must perform identical calculations simultaneously, a machine that lags behind or surges ahead by even a millisecond can be presumed to have erred *(page 80)*.

The information manipulated by the computers comes to

During ascent, four computers analyze data from redundant sensors aboard the shuttle in order to agree on commands for the spacecraft's main engines and movable external control surfaces. In the illustration at right, numbers representing the shuttle's changing pitch arrive at the MDMs from each of the four rate gyros.

Every 40 milliseconds, in answer to queries from the four PASS computers, the MDMs pass the readings over data buses to each of these computers as well as to the backup computer, which participates no further in the process unless switched into the system by the crew.

The PASS computers independently process all four sensor readings according to rules, shared by the computers, that select the larger of the two middle values as best representing the shuttle's actual changing pitch. Based on this determination, the four computers prepare identical commands for main-engine actuators to correct the shuttle's attitude and keep it on course *(pages 82-83)*.

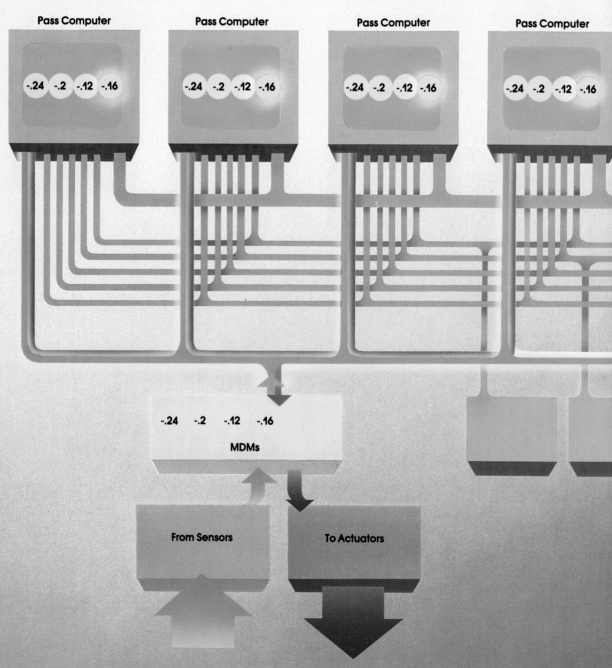

them over data buses in the form of measurements taken by hundreds of sensors on watch throughout the vehicle. Because of minor but unavoidable variations among sensors, data from one rarely matches that from another. The PASS uses special rules to select the best of the values, ensuring that the four primary computers base their calculations on the same sensor data. The resulting commands are passed from each computer to corresponding mechanical actuators — also redundant — that help control the shuttle in flight.

The mediator between the computers at one end of the data bus and the sensors and shuttle machinery at the other is the multiplexer-demultiplexer, a small computer in its own right. There are two MDMs for each of the shuttle's flight-control data buses. (For simplicity, a single box representing all data-bus MDMs is shown here.) They are responsible for translating sensor data into digital form, which the computers can interpret, and for passing the computers' orders to the shuttle's electronics and machinery for action.

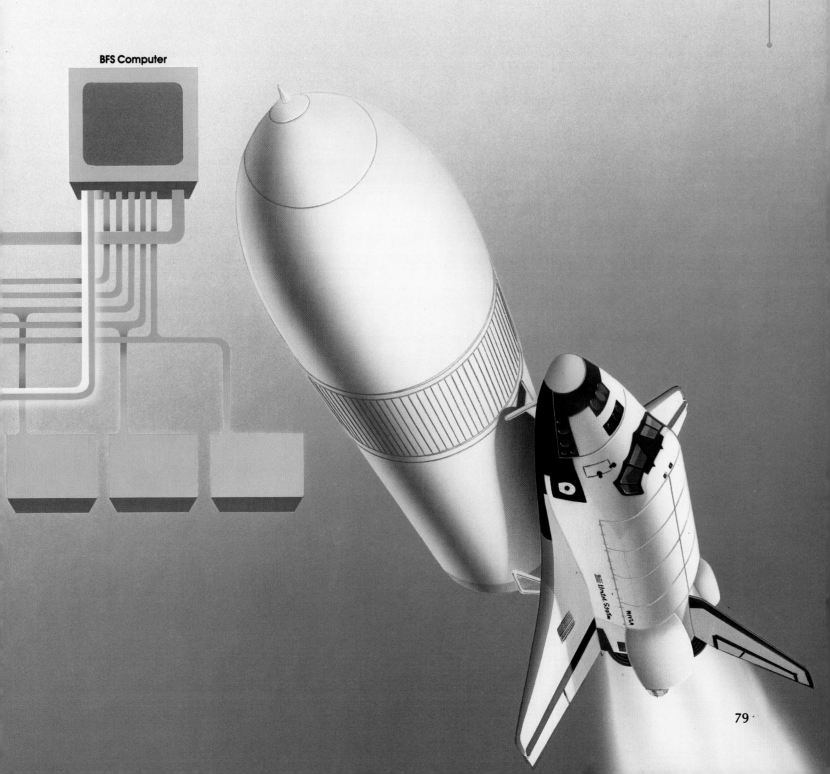

BFS Computer

Keeping the Computers on Schedule

All four PASS computers must not only work the same problem *(pages 78-79)*, but they must complete their calculations within one millisecond of one another. The PASS operating system is responsible for keeping the four computers in step through a process called synchronization. Each GPC contains a clock whose pendulum is a rapidly vibrating crystal. As accurate as these clocks may be, they inevitably run at slightly different rates. To overcome this divergence, the software synchronizes the four PASS GPCs whenever they send or receive data or when they branch to a new software module — about 350 times per second. On each of these occasions, the GPCs pause to exchange special codes over lines reserved

for this activity *(orange)*, then proceed with processing.

If a GPC sends a three-bit error code — 010, in this example — or fails to transmit either an error code or a task-completed code (001) within four milliseconds, the other three GPCs rule the computer faulty. The computers automatically sever communications with the delinquent computer and alert the crew to the problem *(right)*. (Aboard the shuttle, the red lights in the drawing actually appear white, and green lights are unlit, dark spaces.) The offending computer continues to operate independently until manually switched off — a safeguard against software bugs that might command the GPCs to shut each other off automatically.

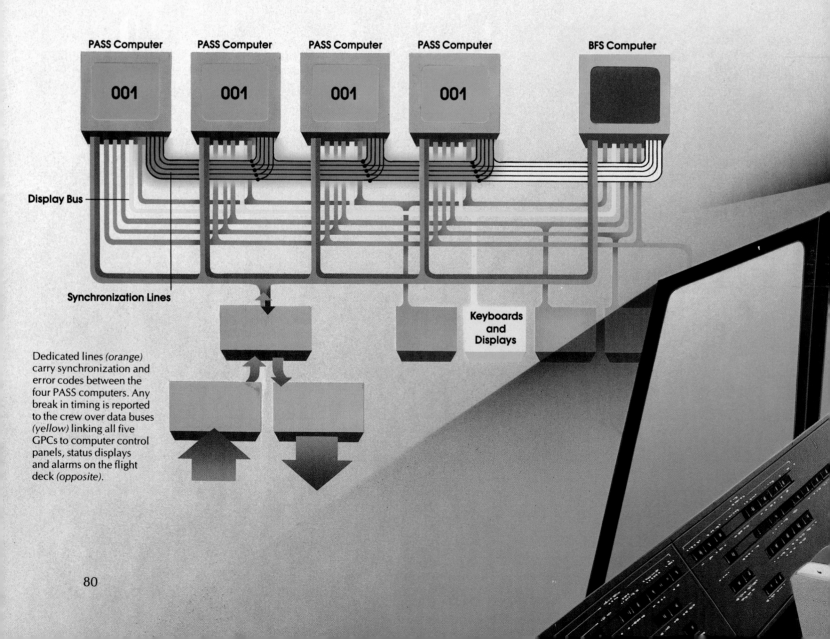

PASS Computer 001 **PASS Computer** 001 **PASS Computer** 001 **PASS Computer** 001 **BFS Computer**

Display Bus

Synchronization Lines

Keyboards and Displays

Dedicated lines *(orange)* carry synchronization and error codes between the four PASS computers. Any break in timing is reported to the crew over data buses *(yellow)* linking all five GPCs to computer control panels, status displays and alarms on the flight deck *(opposite)*.

Red lights on this annunciator panel, positioned above the shuttle commander's seat, indicate a synchronization failure in which GPCs 1, 2 and 4 report that GPC 3 has fallen out of step. From GPC 3's viewpoint, all the others are in error. In reality, GPC 3 is the culprit, as shown by the 010 error code in the center of the five boxes drawn below the annunciator to represent the shuttle's computers.

In this unlikely scenario, the cockpit annunciator shows a deadlock between GPCs 1 and 2 and GPCs 3 and 4, each pair reporting that the others have lost synchronization. If the deadlock threatened the shuttle, the mission commander or the pilot would press a red button on his control stick. Instantly, GPC 5, the backup flight system computer, would take over for the four PASS machines.

Passing Orders down the Line

Rudder

Elevon

Main Engine Exhausts

Body Flap

During the shuttle's ascent to orbit, its aero-dynamic control surfaces — rudder, elevons and body flap — do not steer the craft. Instead, the shuttle is kept on course by a computer-governed hydraulic actuator system *(right)*, which aims the exhaust from the main engines in order to steer the vehicle.

By synchronizing their actions, PASS computers are able to agree on orders destined for the shuttle's flight control surfaces, speed brakes and other mechanical components. These commands may travel only a few hundred feet, from one end of the shuttle to the other, but there is a chance that they could arrive at the end of their journey altered by electronic interference from some unexpected source.

To guard against the danger of orders being misinterpreted, each computer's commands are transmitted separately and combined into a single order only at the last moment. As shown below in a simplified illustration of the system that steers the shuttle by redirecting engine exhaust, a typical mechanical installation aboard the craft includes four intermediary actuators, each executing the command of a single PASS computer. Sensors permit a degree of variation among orders but shunt aside any with results that fall outside preestablished limits. A main actuator — in this case, a piston — then combines the intermediaries' efforts into a single response.

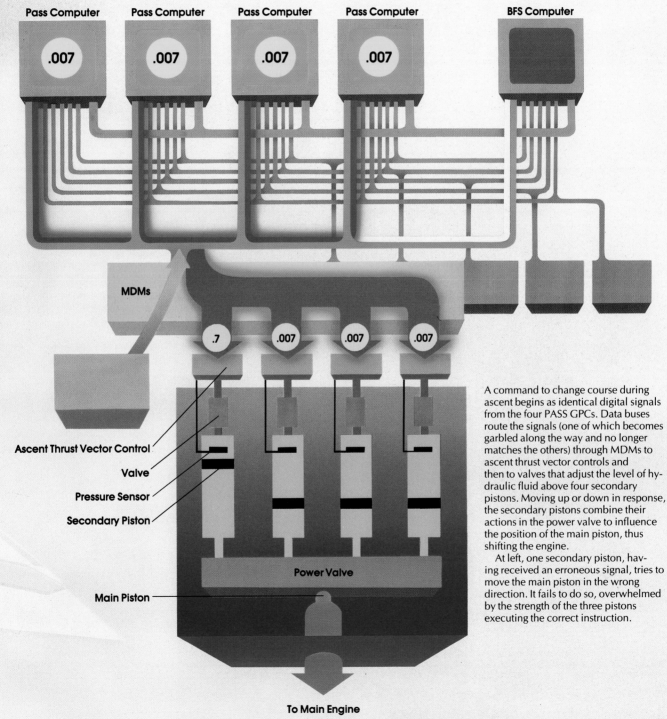

A command to change course during ascent begins as identical digital signals from the four PASS GPCs. Data buses route the signals (one of which becomes garbled along the way and no longer matches the others) through MDMs to ascent thrust vector controls and then to valves that adjust the level of hydraulic fluid above four secondary pistons. Moving up or down in response, the secondary pistons combine their actions in the power valve to influence the position of the main piston, thus shifting the engine.

At left, one secondary piston, having received an erroneous signal, tries to move the main piston in the wrong direction. It fails to do so, overwhelmed by the strength of the three pistons executing the correct instruction.

Reconnaissance by Proxy

The place was Pad 12, Cape Canaveral, in the hot, muggy predawn hours of July 22, 1962. The occasion was the launch of America's first interplanetary probe, *Mariner 1,* bound for Venus. Oran W. Nicks, NASA's director of lunar and planetary programs, ordinarily monitored launches from inside the blockhouse control room. But as the senior official present that morning, he had drawn the duty of hosting two VIP visitors from Capitol Hill, Congressmen James Fulton of Pennsylvania and Joseph Karth of Minnesota. Fulton, flamboyant and strong-willed, insisted on observing the launch firsthand, to glory in the fire and thunder. So, in defiance of the range safety rules, Nicks found himself waiting out the countdown with his companions on the roof of the blockhouse at nearby Pad 14, less than a mile from the Atlas/Agena rocket that was to send *Mariner 1* on its way.

The view, at any rate, was breathtaking. There stood the rocket, Nicks remembers, "poised and erect in the night sky, a great gleaming white projectile lit by searchlights so intense that their beams seemed like blue-white guywires." At the moment of lift-off, 4:22 a.m., he and his companions could feel the rumble of the engines. During the fiery ascent, they could follow the trail of the exhaust as the launcher arced over the Atlantic. And, at precisely four minutes and 50 seconds after lift-off, they could see the explosion and the flaming wreckage that lit up the sky.

"What happened?" asked Congressman Karth, who had never attended a launch before. Nicks, hoping against hope that *Mariner 1* had somehow managed to separate cleanly from its booster before the fireball appeared, thought it more likely that the rocket had gone off course for some reason and had been destroyed by the range-safety officer.

Fulton insisted that Nicks and Karth drive immediately with him to Pad 12 so that he could fill his pockets with bits of wire and other scraps from the launch as souvenirs for visitors from his home district. It was, therefore, quite some time before Nicks could join his disheartened engineers at the Cape's all-night cafeteria, where they were comparing notes, and where it soon became all too clear what had occurred.

Mariner 1 had indeed died in the fireball, the victim of a chance failure compounded by a tiny programming flaw. First, one of the antennas on the Atlas was unable to lock onto the signal, making it impossible for the rocket to receive guidance information from the ground. That in itself might not have been fatal, since the Atlas carried a backup guidance system that was to take over in such a situation and continue the launch. But there was the rub: A programmer had put a period into the backup guidance software where he should have put a comma. Somehow, despite months of debugging and testing the program, no one had ever noticed the error, which made the rocket turn sharply left and down. America's first effort at interplanetary space flight had foundered because of a typo.

Fortunately, the life of *Mariner 1,* however brief, was not prophetic. Despite

rocky beginnings, the space probes that followed proved ever more productive and reliable, leading in 1976 to Viking's stark panoramas of the Martian plains and culminating in the 1980s with Voyager's stunning views of Jupiter, Saturn and Uranus. The accomplishments of these unmanned spacecraft owed a great deal to the engineers who designed and operated them, but they were indebted perhaps even more to the increasingly capable computers that have accompanied the probes on their journeys.

A NEW LEVEL OF DEMANDS

The differences between manned and unmanned spacecraft go much deeper than the presence or absence of astronauts, and nowhere are these differences more evident than in the kinds of computers each carries. To begin with, computers on unmanned spacecraft must be designed for a longer life span than their counterparts on manned vehicles: An unmanned spacecraft on a journey to the far reaches of the solar system may have to operate for a decade or more. Repair is impossible, so the computers aboard have to be extraordinarily dependable.

Just as important, an interplanetary probe must shoulder much of the responsibility for its own guidance and control. Distances between planets make it impossible to guide the spacecraft through a planetary encounter with minute-by-minute instructions from Mission Control. A radio signal from Earth, traveling at the speed of light, takes nearly 20 minutes to make the 200-million-mile trip to Mars. Jupiter is 40 minutes away, Uranus two hours and 45 minutes. Issuing navigation instructions from Earth would be like a football coach trying to communicate with his team by mail: The game would be over before he could call his first play. Indeed, if trouble arose, the spacecraft could be tumbling irretrievably out of control before its electronic cry for help ever reached home. Thus, it is up to the computers aboard a probe to keep its antenna pointed at Earth, to correct the vehicle's course toward its destination and to point scientific instruments at the objective.

As well as being self-reliant, the computers on unmanned missions must be compact, lightweight and frugal with electricity. Interplanetary spacecraft are powered either by solar cells or by small radioisotope thermoelectric generators (RTGs), which convert heat from the decaying isotopes into electricity. These power sources last for many years, but neither produces more than a few hundred watts.

Consequently, while computers aboard manned spacecraft have generally been adapted from commercially available machines, those built into unmanned space probes have been designed from scratch to meet the special challenges of interplanetary flight, a process dominated by a unique institution: the Jet Propulsion Laboratory (JPL) in Pasadena, California.

JPL began in 1936 as the Guggenheim Aeronautical Laboratory, California Institute of Technology (GALCIT); it consisted of a band of six student rocket enthusiasts guided by the eminent Hungarian-born physicist Theodore von Kármán. Though young and inexperienced, von Kármán's crew did first-rate research. Their advances in the theory and practice of solid- and liquid-fueled rocketry, especially after the start of World War II, rank with the breakthroughs made earlier by experimenters under the father of the German V-2, Wernher von Braun. By 1944, GALCIT had attracted such favorable notice that it was renamed the Jet Propulsion Laboratory and expanded into a full-fledged research organization, operated by the California Institute of Technology for the Army Ordnance Corps.

The laboratory's prime responsibility at that time lay in developing missiles for military use. But space beckoned. In the late 1940s, JPL engineers launched the WAC Corporal sounding rocket, the first man-made object to escape Earth's atmosphere. In late 1957, the laboratory built *Explorer 1*, which was launched into space aboard a Jupiter C rocket developed by von Braun's team at Huntsville, Alabama. And on January 1, 1959, JPL became a major contractor to the National Aeronautics and Space Administration.

Those early years were anxious ones for America's space program. Not only had the Soviet Union beaten the United States into orbit with *Sputnik I* in 1957, but it pulled ahead in manned space flight when cosmonaut Yuri Gagarin made his pioneering orbit of Earth in April 1961. Furthermore, the Soviets had begun reconnoitering the planets, attempting missions to Mars and Venus that engineers at JPL could only dream of. True, both of the Soviet Mars launches failed in October 1960, as did one of their two Venus launches the following February. But the second Venus launch succeeded: The Soviet's *Venera 1* was the first spacecraft to leave the environs of Earth. At the end of May 1961, *Venera 1* flew by Venus at a distance of 62,000 miles.

RISING TO THE CHALLENGE

That was too much for JPL director William H. Pickering. Shortly after Gagarin's flight in 1961, he chartered an in-house study to come up with a strategy for the laboratory that would help restore national honor. The authors of this study agreed that the laboratory's efforts should be reoriented around NASA's goal of being first on the moon, and that JPL's objectives should be chosen with national prestige as the most important criterion. As one JPL senior staff member said, "To my mind, a billion-dollar-a-year space program aimed at gaining purely scientific information about outer space is a waste beyond comprehension." Fortunately, JPL had two projects in the works that would fill the bill, Ranger and Surveyor. Both probes looked toward the moon: Ranger to examine the surface at close range while the spacecraft dived toward its destruction, and Surveyor to make a soft landing on the moon and take soil samples and various other measurements to understand the moon's surface characteristics. On May 25, 1961, the same day President Kennedy announced Project Apollo, NASA issued a new flight plan that listed JPL's lunar missions as ventures in direct support of landing men on the moon.

Ranger, as the less ambitious project of the two, came first, and it would prove to be a trial by fire for JPL. Ranger's mission actually was twofold. The explicit goal of the program was to scout suitable landing sites for Apollo. At that time, no one could be certain whether the lunar surface would support a space vehicle or whether the astronauts would sink helplessly into deep layers of dust: Before the probe crashed into the moon kamikaze-style, Ranger would show the surface in unprecedented detail with a stream of television pictures, which JPL scientists hoped would indicate the solidity of the lunar surface.

Ranger's second, more diffuse assignment was to demonstrate that technologies needed for later interplanetary missions were practical, though doing so would make the spacecraft unnecessarily complicated. For example, Ranger was to use solar cells for power, even though batteries would have sufficed for the 66-hour flight to the moon. And it was to have an ultrasensitive, or high-gain, antenna for communicating with the mission controllers back at JPL, although a journey of a quarter of a million miles could have been accomplished using a less sensitive device. The difficulty with a high-gain antenna lay in its directionality, which required that Ranger maintain an unvarying attitude to keep the antenna pointed directly at Earth. If it became even slightly misaimed, communications with the probe would be lost. Furthermore, cameras and other instruments for observing the planets would benefit from a stable platform.

For all these reasons, Ranger would use a technique known as three-axis stabilization to keep itself from pitching, rolling or yawing in flight. Ranger was to orient itself in much the same way that a mariner does with a sextant — locking onto the sun, a star or a planet. But for Ranger to find its celestial signposts without human assistance and to use the information to keep itself properly aligned would require highly sophisticated instrumentation and also a full array of attitude-control sensors and thrusters.

And if these complications were not enough, Ranger would also carry its own electronic command center. It would serve primarily as a backup to flight controllers on the ground, who would not be inconvenienced by the 1.3-second travel time of a radio signal from Earth to the moon. This 11-pound central computer and sequencer was an outgrowth of similar devices used in JPL's rocket designs. Despite the name, the sequencer was more of a glorified digital timer than a computer. It lacked a central processing unit (CPU), the heart of a computer. Moreover, it could follow only a single set of instructions, wired into its memory during assembly. For this reason, the machine was known as a fixed sequencer.

Yet, for the early 1960s, Ranger's sequencer was a marvel of automation. From a few hours before launch, an internal clock counted seconds backward to zero, the point at which the spacecraft was to crash into the moon. En route, the sequencer controlled activity aboard the spacecraft according to a schedule installed well in advance of the mission. For example, the device controlled the spacecraft's orientation with the three-axis stabilization system, managed the propulsion firing intervals during trajectory correction maneuvers and turned on the cameras as the probe neared the moon.

Without rebuilding the sequencer, the order of events could not be changed, though mission controllers on the ground could assume command of the spacecraft. In addition, controllers could pass to the sequencer four crucial pieces of information for a maneuver called the midcourse correction. Its purpose was to adjust Ranger's trajectory so that the vehicle would strike the moon as planned. To accomplish this maneuver, sequencer designers left blank four locations in the machine's memory. Shortly before the midcourse correction was to occur, the blanks would be filled in with numbers, transmitted from Earth, which the sequencer would use to fire Ranger's rockets, refining the spacecraft's course.

After months of working at breakneck pace, JPL had *Ranger 1* ready to go by the summer of 1961. But the launch, on August 23, was disappointing. A faulty upper-stage booster failed to kick the spacecraft into its proper trajectory toward the moon. *Ranger 1* quickly spiraled back into Earth's atmosphere and disintegrated. Much the same thing happened to *Ranger 2,* launched three months later.

Ranger 3, after a seemingly perfect launch on January 26, 1962, began to drift off course: Later analysis revealed a programming error that turned the spacecraft's path into the mirror image of what it should have been. JPL engineers successfully radioed course corrections to the vehicle, but two days later, just as *Ranger 3* was altering course for final approach to the moon, its radio signal began to fluctuate wildly. A failure in the sequencer had allowed the spacecraft to start tumbling, aiming the antenna away from Earth. Unable to regain control of the spacecraft, JPL engineers could only watch helplessly as *Ranger 3* missed the moon by 23,000 miles and headed into solar orbit, its cameras madly recording images of empty space.

Ranger 4 offered more hope — at first. The launch and flight were perfect: A midcourse correction had not even been necessary. But as the spacecraft approached the moon, the master clock in the sequencer failed. *Ranger 4* crashed on the dark side of the moon on April 26, 1962 — without sending a single picture of the surface. "All we've got," groused one NASA official about the Ranger program to date, "is an idiot with a radio signal."

MARINER: A SUCCESS AT LAST

Project Ranger's litany of failure teemed with implications for another space-exploration project at JPL — the Mariner probes of Earth's nearest neighbor, Venus. Similar in design to Ranger, Mariner was developed at about the same time by a different JPL team. The probe was to be America's first full-fledged interplanetary spacecraft. It would venture far enough from Earth to require the technology that, as unnecessary embellishment, had caused most of Ranger's woes.

The distance the probes had to travel to Venus — 45 million miles — necessitated high-gain antennas. And with a delay of up to 14 minutes between transmission and receipt of a command from Earth, ground controllers would play backup to the on-board sequencer. In other words, a close cousin of the sequencer that had already failed twice was to be given full responsibility for a mission.

The Mariner program did not seem like much of a respite from the string of humiliations that had marked Ranger's progress. The short, incendiary flight of *Mariner 1,* which provided Congressman Fulton with his pocketfuls of souvenirs, occurred just three months after the fourth Ranger died, hardly a good omen. But the launch of *Mariner 2* on August 27, 1962, finally broke the jinx. On December 14, 1962, after 108 days of near-flawless operation, *Mariner 2* passed within 21,000 miles of the surface of Venus. Among its many revelations was the fact that temperatures on the planet's cloud-obscured surface reached 800° F. Far from being the planet of steamy swamps that was depicted in science fiction, Venus was a seething hell.

Mariner 2 was a tremendous morale booster for JPL. Not only was it America's first success with an unmanned probe, but perhaps best of all, in the view of

1 As Venus rotates, the orbiting radar mapper maneuvers itself to beam a series of microwave pulses obliquely through the planet's cloud cover, revealing the hidden surface. On-board computers record the travel times and frequencies of the echoes for later transmission to Earth. Shown exaggerated for clarity, the areas covered by the pulses overlap to form a swath 10,000 miles long and 15 miles wide.

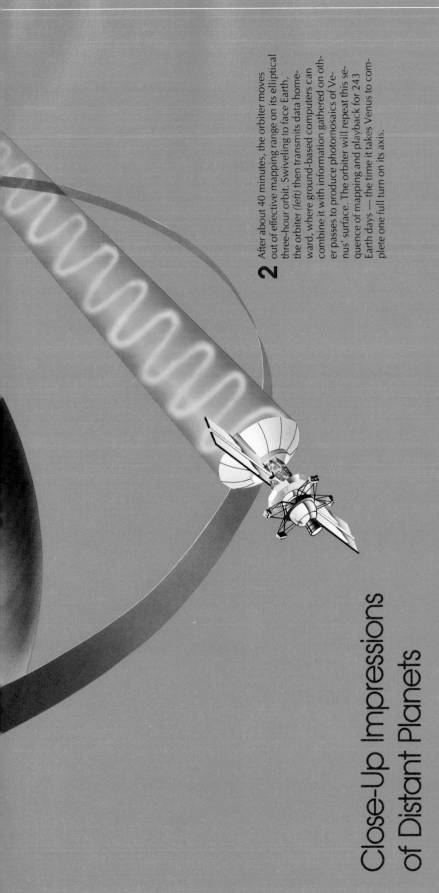

4

Close-Up Impressions of Distant Planets

By its very nature, the course of space exploration is the reverse of that taken by generations of terrestrial explorers. Unable at first to make detailed observations and measurements on the surface of planetary bodies, space scientists have gleaned knowledge of the planets from fly-by reconnaissance craft, such as the Mariner probes to Mars and Venus and the Voyager flights to more distant planets (pages 103-113). These missions constitute the first phase of planetary study: By returning preliminary information on the characteristics of a planet's atmosphere and general indications of its surface topography, they have allowed researchers to tailor instruments and experiments for later flights.

Shown here and on the following pages are probes that are scheduled to carry out the second, or exploratory, phase of investigation. During this stage, scientists will seek to determine such things as the dynamics of a planet's atmosphere and its geological history. Mapping the surface of a planet requires that a probe remain in orbit long enough to record data from at least 70 percent of the surface, with enough resolution to pick out major features such as faults, folds, cones and lava flows.

For bodies with little or no atmosphere, optical instruments are adequate. But to get a look at planets or satellites with dense atmospheric cover, other technologies will be required. The planned Venus orbiter shown above, for instance, is designed to carry a radar system that can

pierce the planet's thick clouds of carbon dioxide and sulfuric acid.

An ordinary radar would map a section of the planet's surface by transmitting a single microwave pulse through the clouds. Depending on the terrain within the radar's field of view, the pulse will scatter in many directions. Capturing enough of these echoes from a single radar pulse to provide a detailed map would require an antenna — or aperture, as radar engineers call it — several hundred yards in diameter. Such a structure is clearly impractical for the Venus probe or any other. The solution is a system of data collection called a synthetic-aperture radar (SAR).

Used for years in military reconnaissance aircraft, SAR will permit the Venus orbiter's antenna, which is only a few yards in diameter, to function as though it were hundreds of times larger. To accomplish this, not one radar pulse but hundreds of them will be used to map the area that could be covered by an individual pulse of a conventional, or real-aperture, radar. The probe's antenna, being relatively small, will capture only a few echoes from each pulse. They will be recorded and another pulse transmitted. In the meantime, the orbiter will have moved along its trajectory, and echoes from any surface feature struck by successive pulses will differ slightly. On Earth, the accumulated data will be processed by computer into images as rich in detail as those produced by a real-aperture radar system with an antenna several hundred yards wide.

2 After about 40 minutes, the orbiter moves out of effective mapping range on its elliptical three-hour orbit. Swiveling to face Earth, the orbiter (left) then transmits data homeward, where ground-based computers can combine it with information gathered on other passes to produce photomosaics of Venus' surface. The orbiter will repeat this sequence of mapping and playback for 243 Earth days — the time it takes Venus to complete one full turn on its axis.

Penetrating a Planet's Secrets

Probes such as the surface-mapping Venus orbiter on the preceding pages can gain an abundance of information at a distance. But this strategy will not suffice for studies of the composition and dynamics of a planet's atmosphere or the composition of smaller bodies such as comets and asteroids (box). Such work calls for a closeup look by an entry probe, which compared with an orbiter will have a very short life-span. Subjected to atmospheric pressures, chemically corrosive clouds and high temperatures, entry devices may cease to function within a few hours.

A planned mission to Jupiter — scheduled for the early 1990s — will make the best of these trade-offs with a two-part spacecraft (below, left): Several months before arrival, the craft will separate into an orbiter, which will circle Jupiter and tour its moons, and an entry probe, which will head directly toward the planet. Coinciding with the orbiter's closest approach — 120,000 miles or so above the clouds — the entry probe will descend into the planet's upper atmosphere. Various instruments will measure such characteristics as temperature, density, energy exchange and chemical makeup, transmitting the data to the orbiter overhead. After about an hour, meteorological interference, intense radiation and increasing distance will sever the communications link, and eventually the entry probe will be crushed by atmospheric pressure more than 100 times that of Earth. The orbiter, for its part, will continue to survey Jupiter and its moons for two years or more.

En route to a rendezvous with Jupiter, an unmanned craft (above, left) will split into two parts: a remote orbiter, which will circle the planet, and an entry probe designed to perform the first direct sampling of Jupiter's atmosphere. Five months later, the entry probe will calibrate its cargo of scientific instruments and plunge into the Jovian clouds at more than 100,000 miles per hour, burning away much of its heat shield (left, 0-240 miles penetration). As it continues its predetermined

path of descent, the probe will open its pilot parachute, carrying off the top cover and popping the main parachute. The entry probe will then eject the remains of the heat shield (250 miles penetration). For the next hour, the probe will transmit instrument data to the remote orbiter (above, right). After this data-gathering phase, the entry probe will be silenced, ultimately succumbing to being crushed by atmospheric pressure and to heat intense enough to melt the little craft.

0-240 Miles

360 Miles

251 Miles

250 Miles

245 Miles

A Spike in the Ice

Because comets are among the best preserved products of the processes that formed the solar system, scientists are eager to determine the chemical composition and physical properties of a cometary nucleus through the use of penetrator probes. The penetrator at left, equipped with a variety of instruments, is designed to be deployed by a transport spacecraft, which will in turn relay the findings to Earth. Planted a few feet deep, the penetrator will reach through the comet's superficial crust to the eons-old matter below.

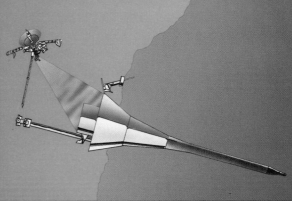

JPL's director, Pickering, it pulled the United States abreast of the Soviet Union in planetary exploration.

MORE OF THE SAME FROM RANGER

In the meantime, however, the Ranger program had resumed its hapless ways. On October 18, 1962, *Ranger 5* suffered a loss of power from its solar cells shortly after launch. Blindly turning cartwheels, it missed the moon by 450 miles and was interred in solar orbit.

The failure of *Ranger 5* brought the project to a halt for more than a year while JPL redesigned the spacecraft and painstakingly tested the modifications. Even so, *Ranger 6,* launched January 30, 1964, was the most disappointing yet. After a successful lift-off and a perfect midcourse maneuver, the craft maintained alignment without a hitch. Mission controllers eagerly awaited the first close-up portraits of the moon — but the probe's cameras never came to life. "I never want to go through an experience like this again," said an ashen Pickering. "Never."

The press had a field day. Jokes about forgotten lens caps made the rounds. Comic-strip detective Dick Tracy solved the mystery while on a moon cruise in a friend's space coupe: "It's easy to see why the cameras failed," he said as he investigated the wreckage. "They were never turned on." And he was right. The failure was quickly traced to an electrical discharge that had damaged the high-voltage power supplies as *Ranger 6* had passed through the upper atmosphere. For once, the sequencer was not to blame.

NASA mounted an all-encompassing inquiry into the Ranger program, going beyond the hardware failures to question the design philosophy of the Ranger spacecraft and even the competence of the JPL designers, especially those on the sequencer team. Congress launched its own investigation, clouding the future of the laboratory.

After months of review accompanied by rigorous retesting and analysis, the effort to hit the moon resumed. *Ranger 7* was launched successfully on July 28, made its midcourse connection shortly thereafter and headed right for the target: Estimated time of arrival was 6:25 a.m., July 31. A little after six in the morning, two of the spacecraft's six cameras responded to the sequencer and began to warm up. As soon as *Ranger 7* reported this event by telemetry, cheers erupted from the audience of reporters and VIPs waiting in the auditorium of the JPL.

At 6:10, *Ranger 7's* remaining four cameras began to warm up, then signals representing the first pictures arrived. The flight announcer's voice seemed to race along with events, counting down the minutes to impact and reveling in the long-overdue success: "Two minutes, all systems operating. Preliminary analysis shows pictures being received. One minute to impact. Excellent. Excellent. Signals to the end. IMPACT!"

Ranger 7's telemetry, humming over the JPL loudspeakers, gave way to the soft hiss of interplanetary static while the engineers and scientists in the laboratory exulted. Some JPL employees tossed papers into the air. Some wept. "For those of us who had lived Ranger for so long, it was a kind of spiritual happening," recalls one JPL staff member. There would be other successes at the laboratory. There would be missions that were more advanced and scientific investigations that were more fruitful. Yet for many of the JPL staffers who were present that day, the triumph of *Ranger 7* was an experience that no other project has matched.

Over the next couple of years, sequencers performed admirably on several Ranger and Mariner probes, but the device first made a star of an unmanned probe with *Surveyor 1*. On June 1, 1966, this craft descended gently to the moon and touched down in the crater Oceanus Procellarum, the first time that a spacecraft had ever achieved a soft landing on another celestial body. *Surveyor 1* proved that the moon's surface could indeed support a spacecraft. During 28 days of impeccable operation in the crater, the sequencer aboard *Surveyor 1* received thousands of commands from Earth and executed them without error. It also transmitted 11,240 lunar landscapes to Earth. In September 1967, the sequencer aboard *Surveyor 5* helped turn near-disaster into success. After discovering a fuel leak during the midflight phase of the mission, controllers at JPL were able to radio to the probe a modified sequence of commands that let *Surveyor 5* descend to the lunar surface as if nothing had gone wrong.

As impressive as these feats were, they only emphasized the limitations of existing sequencers. The devices were just too simple-minded and too rigid for the kinds of missions that JPL was planning next. Neil Herman, head of JPL's sequencer team for Mariner, was convinced that the time had come to take the next step: a sequencer with additional memory that could be reprogrammed even after a mission was under way.

He made his pitch as JPL was planning a tandem flight for *Mariners* 6 and 7, to take place in 1969. Known collectively as Mariner Mars 69, the twin spacecraft were to fly past Mars and photograph extended areas of its surface. Sending two spacecraft was insurance: If one failed, the other might complete the mission. But if all went well, Herman argued, a reprogrammable sequencer would offer a unique opportunity. Suppose the fly-by of *Mariner* 6 uncovered something unexpected. Then *Mariner 7*, trailing a few days behind, could be given new instructions to investigate the matter. Since *Mariners* 6 and 7 were to be bigger and heavier than any previous probe, sequencer engineers could use their share of the additional weight and roominess for a more capable sequencer.

Herman's logic was unassailable, and work began on the new sequencer almost immediately. Some 30 months later, it had been built, tested and made ready for duty. The new device had 128 words of memory and, as Herman had advocated, was completely reprogrammable. No instructions were to be wired permanently into the new sequencer, as they had been in its predecessor. To handle this increased capability, the sequencer required a central processing unit. The addition of a CPU brought the sequencer one step closer to becoming a computer. Yet it had only a limited arithmetic and logic capability, sufficient for counting off the passing seconds but hardly enough to qualify the machine as a fully functional computer.

The new sequencer weighed a hefty 26 pounds. Even so, there was enough room aboard each of the twin spacecraft to bring an 11-pound fixed sequencer, similar to the one aboard *Mariner 2*, on the trip to Mars, the first instance of computer backup aboard an unmanned space vehicle. For certain critical maneuvers, such as midcourse corrections, the two sequencers would perform the same functions simultaneously, with the programmable sequencer as the prime player. If they agreed in their results, the spacecraft would perform the maneuver. In case of disagreement, the maneuver would be automatically delayed until ground controllers discovered the problem and overriding instructions could be radioed from Earth.

That the Mars-bound sequencer had reprogrammable memory proved invaluable for reasons not clearly foreseen when the sequencer was proposed. As would happen in the effort to send humans into space, the programs that were needed to take the Mariner craft to Mars soon overflowed the new sequencer's expanded memory. Thus it became necessary to divide the programs into segments that mission controllers would load into memory as needed, a solution that would have been impossible without reprogrammable memory.

The trip to Mars began with *Mariner 6's* launch in February 1969. *Mariner 7* followed a month later. The flexibility of the new sequencer paid off dramatically. As *Mariner 6* was completing a successful fly-by of the planet, its companion, *Mariner 7,* suddenly began tumbling wildly through space, a problem later traced to a small explosion in the probe's storage battery. Although JPL engineers were able to contact the spacecraft and reorient it, the gyrations had knocked the camera platform out of alignment. *Mariner 7's* entire Martian encounter was in jeopardy; the spacecraft might produce nothing but pictures of empty space.

Working quickly, however, JPL engineers radioed new orders to *Mariner 7's* sequencer: Turn on the wide-angle camera earlier than planned, then pan the camera slowly across the heavens. Eventually, the camera picked up Mars, allowing the controllers to re-aim the cameras. That feat accomplished, the crew on the ground rechecked the attitude-control and power systems, the scientific instruments and even the sequencer itself to make certain that all was well aboard the spacecraft.

NEW VIEWS OF AN OLD NEIGHBOR

Together, the Mariner Mars 69 spacecraft returned 201 images of the Red Planet, representing approximately 10 percent of its surface. For scientists, the pictures were a revelation. Whereas the handful of blurred images made four years earlier by *Mariner 4* had seemed to show a cratered planet remarkably like the moon, this new coverage revealed that Mars also possessed deserts on a grand scale, as well as tracts of jumbled ridges and valleys, often without any craters at all. The planet even had polar caps of dry ice — frozen carbon dioxide, the predominant component of the Martian atmosphere.

Even more startling revelations were in store from the next Mariner flights, launched in 1971. Known collectively as Mariner Mars 71, *Mariners 8* and *9* would orbit Mars and map the surface in detail. Indeed, they would be the first of mankind's creations to orbit another planet. A 300-pound-thrust engine was added to the basic Mariner spacecraft to slow the probe and settle it into orbit once it reached Mars. Major improvements were also made in the television cameras and in the attitude-control system. In the reprogrammable sequencer, memory capacity was increased still further.

Once again, the programmability of Mariner's sequencer turned out to be crucial for the success of the mission. As if to remind the Mariner scientists that rockets could still be treacherous, *Mariner 8* died early, on May 5, 1971, when a faulty booster failed to lift the spacecraft into Earth orbit. *Mariner 9,* launched successfully on May 30, 1971, would somehow have to carry out a two-spacecraft mission on its own. Back at JPL, scientists and programmers went to work devising a hybrid sequence of observations that would salvage as much of the original plan as possible.

BILLOWS OF YELLOW DUST

Then the new plan also had to be scrapped. In late September of 1971, with *Mariner 9* two thirds of the way to Mars, a bright yellow cloud appeared in the southern hemisphere of Mars — the worst dust storm ever recorded. Within two weeks it had spread to engulf the whole planet. And by November 13, when the spacecraft finally slid into orbit, the surface was totally obscured. *Mariner 9* had to wait three months for the dust storm to subside. During that time, mission controllers reprogrammed the spacecraft for a reconnaissance mode, which included global scans of the planet on each orbit, followed by efforts to zero in on targets in relatively clear areas.

When the dust cleared, *Mariner 9* was reprogrammed into a mapping mode and during the next nine months redefined Mars for earthlings. The planet revealed itself as a crazy quilt of geological activity dwarfing anything to be found on Earth. Olympus Mons, a massive volcano with a base the size of Missouri, rises 15 miles into the sky, almost three times the height of Mount Everest. Valles Marineris (Valley of the Mariners), a chasm four miles deep, up to 400 miles wide and nearly 3,000 miles long, makes a gulley of the Grand Canyon. And perhaps most astonishing were the sinuous, braided channels meandering across the face of Mars, like river valleys. Seemingly, water had once been abundant on the now-arid surface of Mars.

If additional confirmation of the value of programmable memory was needed, it came in the form of a Russian Mars probe launched at about the same time. Known as *Mars 2,* its sequencer was not programmable; the cameras went through their preset sequence before the dust storm had abated, and they returned very little of interest.

The last Mariner probe, number 10 in the series, took off on November 3, 1973, on a journey that would prove to be the most satisfying demonstration yet of Neil Herman's programmable sequencer. The mission itself was an interplanetary bank shot that any pool shark might envy. Blasting off from Earth, *Mariner 10* took advantage of a rare alignment of planets that allowed it to travel past the moon and Venus, then to swing by Mercury, in a looping orbit around the sun that would carry it by Mercury twice again.

As before, instructions for the mission were divided into segments and radioed to the sequencer's memory as needed. An additional 384 words added to the sequencer's memory allowed JPL controllers to store a skeletal backup program that would permit the spacecraft to complete its mission in a bare-bones fashion should *Mariner 10* lose contact with Earth and be unable to receive the next segment of the flight program. In that event, the sequencer would switch automatically to the backup program.

Mariner 10 accomplished its complex flight plan without missing a beat and revealed much about Mercury. Devoid of an atmosphere to moderate its temperature, the planet was hot enough by day to melt lead and colder than dry ice at night. A cratered surface concealed an Earth-like core of molten iron.

About three years before *Mariner 10's* reconnaissance of Mercury, NASA and JPL had received a green light for an even more ambitious undertaking, called

Viking. This explorer was to revisit Mars, but instead of merely flying by the planet or circling it, Viking was to land there. At a cost of one billion dollars, two missions were to be flown, *Viking 1* and *Viking 2*. Each would consist of a Mars orbiter that would dispatch a lander to the planet's surface. A robot arm on each lander was to scoop samples of Martian soil into a hopper. Machinery inside the lander would pulverize the soil and analyze it for evidence of life, past or present.

It became clear to the Viking design team early on that the sequencers used for the Mariner probes would be inadequate for Viking. The computers would have to perform trajectory calculations for landing, manage the probes' systems, make decisions and generally conduct more complicated command sequences. None of these could be done by a sequencer that was able to count only by ones. Viking would need a true computer.

Neil Herman had assumed leadership for the flight-data system by the time that work began on the Viking command computer subsystem (VCCS), as it was known. The device was a direct descendant of his programmable sequencer design. But in addition to being equipped with more memory and a mathematical whiz of a central processing unit, the Viking computer would be the first such device built at JPL to fully implement the concept of redundancy. When it was finished in 1974, the computer would have two power supplies, two central processors, two memories — two of everything. Except for the busiest phases of the mission, when they would function individually, the two computers would solve problems simultaneously.

This practice of redundancy made the VCCS remarkably resistant to failure — exactly what a flight-control system needs 440 million miles from home. If one of the computers developed a glitch at a critical moment, its task would be switched over instantly to its twin and the procedure would continue without interruption.

So reliable a system could be entrusted with critical functions — firing the rocket engines, for example. Whenever a Ranger or Mariner spacecraft had needed to correct its course or perform any other maneuver, calculations had been made on the ground and commands radioed to the sequencer: Starting at such and such a time, fire your engines for 59 seconds and then stop. With Viking, however, midcourse corrections and insertion into orbit around Mars were to be controlled by the on-board computer. The flight engineers would tell the VCCS only how much extra velocity the spacecraft needed, and the computers would fire engines as long as necessary. Since the VCCS was on the scene, it could correct for small variations in thrust and other anomalies that the engineers on the ground could only guess at. The result was a much greater accuracy in spacecraft navigation.

Viking's computers guided the two orbiters to Mars, and similar devices aboard the landers assisted them gently to the planet's surface. But in the end, Viking found no life on Mars. If anything, the possibility of life on the Red Planet seemed more remote than it had after *Mariner 9's* visit. Neither the Plains of Gold, where the *Viking 1* lander set down in the early morning hours of July 20, 1976, nor the Plains of Utopia, where the *Viking 2* lander set down on September 3, 1976, yielded soil samples containing living organisms.

The mission was nonetheless a technological tour de force. The two orbiters far outlasted the 90-day lifetime promised by JPL. The *Viking 2* orbiter operated until 1978, and the *Viking 1* orbiter did not fall silent until mid-August 1980. Ultimately they returned some 52,000 high-resolution pictures covering 97 percent of the Martian surface, more than mission planners had ever dreamed possible. The landers, after the completion of their initial reconnaissance, were reprogrammed for an extended mission. During the next few years they returned a unique and priceless record of the weather and climate on another world.

TO JUPITER AND BEYOND

Even as Viking was capping the explorations of the inner solar system, planning was well under way at JPL for a two-spacecraft mission, christened Voyager, to the outer solar system — the cold realm of the giant planets Jupiter, Saturn, Uranus and Neptune.

The two Voyager spacecraft, launched in the late summer of 1977, had been assigned to study Jupiter and Saturn as their primary mission. The success of such a journey depended on the computers aboard the twin spacecraft operating properly for at least four years. Saturn, after all, is more than a billion miles away. The demands upon *Voyager 2*, however, would be even greater. The second spacecraft would trail the first by several months, acting as a backup in case disaster befell *Voyager 1*. But if all went well, *Voyager 2* would then take advantage of a rare opportunity. Once every other century or so, Jupiter, Saturn, Uranus and Neptune are aligned in such a way that the gravity of one will fling a spacecraft on to the next. *Voyager 2* would thus go on from Saturn to complete a grand tour of the outer solar system, ultimately passing Neptune in late August of 1989, twelve years after it had departed from Earth.

Such a mission clearly called for more self-reliance, more flexibility and a greater capacity for on-board decision-making than any mission before it. To accomplish that, the Voyager spacecraft carried not one but six computers, paired for redundancy and backup. One set, the command computer subsystem, was to run the spacecraft; it was identical, in its essentials, to the system used on Viking. A second pair of computers maintained the orientation of the spacecraft and pointed its cameras. The third set of computers formatted the data gathered by Voyager so that it could be radioed back to Earth.

The leader of the team that developed the data-formatting computer turned out to be none other than Neil Herman. The flight-data system, he recalled, "was a bigger and more expensive computer than the others, and in flight it was going to require a much, much broader involvement with the scientists who were commanding Voyager." It also incorporated the most advanced semiconductor technology of the mid-1970s and used special electronics designed to survive fierce radiation belts around Jupiter.

LIGHTWEIGHTS AMONG COMPUTERS

Even so, Voyager's computers were considerably less powerful than the machines found on many a desktop. "You can't even compare them," said Herman later. "Voyager was designed 10 years before the IBM PC. We didn't even have a flight-qualified microprocessor back then. In those days a computer took up 100,000 watts of power and roomfuls of equipment. You might buy one of them for the whole lab. But on a spacecraft you're constrained by size and weight."

And yet, he said, "Voyager was an extraordinary piece of equipment." However limited its computers might have been by today's standards, the spacecraft has shown a remarkable ability to adapt to the new and the unexpected. On August 25, 1981, for example, just as Voyager 2 was whipping around Saturn en route to Uranus, a movable platform — to which the spacecraft's cameras and many of its other instruments are attached — abruptly ceased to function. An immobile platform was, for the spacecraft, like having a horrible crick in the neck; the probe was unable to look around at the sights it had come so far to see. Fortunately, the problem had a solution. By programming a series of diagnostic tests into the attitude-control computer, the JPL engineers traced the problem to insufficient lubricant in one of the platform's gears. Soon the overheated components cooled sufficiently to free the gear, and by the time of the Uranus encounter in January 1986, JPL engineers had devised command sequences that minimized the stress on that gear.

The Uranus encounter provided multiple examples of the computer's flexibility. Uranus is so far away that the Voyager programmers had to devise a different way to encode the scientific data being returned to Earth. Just as shouting to a friend as far away as the length of a football field requires deliberate articulation, the farther away Voyager 2 travels, the harder it becomes for tracking stations to hear the probe's signals and the less data can be transmitted in a given amount of time. This problem was already irksome at Saturn. But it would have been crippling at Uranus, 1.7 billion miles away. Pictures, in particular, require millions of bits of data apiece; if nothing had been done, Voyager 2 would have been able to return only a handful of images from Uranus. The solution was to compress the data, so that the same amount could be sent in a shorter time *(pages 112-113)*.

Programmers made other changes to the spacecraft's routines to help it cope with such factors as low light levels at Uranus — the sun illuminates Uranus about as brightly as a full moon shines on Earth. Indeed, before JPL had finished with the spacecraft's brain, it had been substantially rebuilt by remote control. The computer was not the same machine that had left Earth nearly a decade before. And Voyager worked beautifully, returning some 200 pictures a day from Uranus, together with a wealth of other scientific information.

Success was a near thing. On January 20, 1986, four days before *Voyager 2's* closest approach to Uranus, a memory cell failed in one of the flight-data computers — which, as Murphy's law would have it, was the computer dedicated to handling data compression. Pictures were coming back garbled. Richard Rice, one of the two programmers responsible for the flight-data computer, remembers taking his grandchildren to Disneyland that Sunday afternoon. Because of the outing he did not receive word of the problem until later that evening. Unable to sleep, he and fellow programmer Edward Blizzard were at work on the problem by 2 o'clock Monday morning. They had the computer send them what was, in effect, a report on itself. They then compared that report with the original specifications. "It was like looking for a needle in a haystack," Rice says. Luckily, they found the faulty cell — number 453 of 8,192 such cells in the computer's memory — in only half an hour. Rice and Blizzard quickly sent up a set of commands to tell the computer how to work around the failure, and a few hours later, just before the encounter began, the problem was solved.

Voyager proved to be by far the most fruitful of NASA's missions to the planets. "Our Beethoven, Bach and Mozart," was how one JPL engineer praised the project. It returned images of stunning impact: the psychedelic cloudscapes of Jupiter; the volcanic face of the planet's red moon, Io; the butterscotch banding of Saturn and the icy expanse of its rings; the patchwork terrain of Uranus' moon Miranda. The wonder at its discoveries could hardly have been greater if *Voyager 2* had explored not the sun's planets but those of a distant star.

FUTURE PROBES

Precisely what comes next is still unclear. The explosion of the space shuttle *Challenger* on January 28, 1986, put most of the American space program on hold, delaying some previously planned launches by two, three or even four years. But a rich variety of interplanetary missions stand ready to go. These include Mars Observer, a relatively simple spacecraft designed to orbit the Red Planet and track the ebb and flow of water vapor in its atmosphere; the Ulysses mission, a cooperative venture between NASA and the European Space Agency to send a spacecraft into the unexplored regions over the poles of the sun; the Magellan mission, an effort to map the cloud-wrapped surface of Venus with imaging radar; and most especially, the Galileo mission to Jupiter.

The Galileo vehicle actually consists of two parts. The probe section will be dropped into the Jovian atmosphere during the spacecraft's initial approach; during the next hour, until the probe is crushed by the ever-mounting pressure, it will radio back our first direct information about the nature of that violent atmosphere. Meanwhile, the Galileo orbiter will take up residence around the giant planet, in much the same way that *Mariner 9* and the Viking spacecraft settled into orbit around Mars. Over the next 20 months, the orbiter will loop around the giant planet 11 times, investigating its atmosphere and satellites in exquisite closeup detail.

Given the complexity of this mission, it should not be surprising that Galileo will have the largest and most powerful computer network ever to fly on an unmanned spacecraft. Indeed, it will be the first spacecraft to exclusively use modern microprocessor technology. In fact, eight of the nine instruments on board will have their own microprocessors. The command and data systems, which were separate on Voyager, will be combined into one system that has six microprocessors. Attitude and control will be handled by dual computers. And the probe will have its own dual-processor system.

After Galileo, other exploratory ventures call. JPL is currently designing a modular spacecraft known as Mariner Mark II, which will use technology developed for Voyager and Galileo to carry out a variety of missions — if budgets permit. Among the possibilities are a rendezvous with a comet, visits to a series of asteroids and an orbiter/probe mission to Titan, one of Saturn's moons. Meanwhile, the Soviet Union is developing modular spacecraft to visit Mars and the asteroid Vesta.

And finally, of course, there is still *Voyager 2,* drifting steadily toward its rendezvous with Neptune on August 24, 1989. Neptune will be *Voyager 2's* last hurrah: If all goes well, the spacecraft will then head out of the solar system in the general direction of Sirius, the Dog Star, which glitters in the winter sky at the heels of Orion, the hunter. Meanwhile, *Voyager I,* its encounters with Jupiter and Saturn complete, is headed into the summer sky in the general direction of the star Reselhaugue, or Alpha Ophiuchus. For the next few decades, as their signals grow weaker with distance, both should continue to radio back information about the conditions of the interplanetary medium. And then they will fall silent.

It will be another 40,000 years before either comes within a light year of another star, and perhaps a million years before one of them might make a close pass at another planetary system. Our own civilization here on Earth may be long dead by that time. But each Voyager spacecraft carries a 12-inch, gold-plated copper disk encoding some of the sights and sounds of Earth. Perhaps some far-distant intelligent civilization will one day find them. And if so, as they examine these strange, instrument-laden relics of another time and another place, they may gain a glimmer of who we were.

Voyager's Grand Odyssey

The space age has brought astronomers a new and far more effective way of studying our celestial neighbors. Once limited to dim and atmosphere-bleared views in a telescope, they now send unmanned, computerized spacecraft on journeys of millions and sometimes billions of miles for a close-up look at other members of the solar system.

Beginning with the Soviet Union's Venera program in the early 1960s, efforts at planetary reconnaissance have become progressively more ambitious. The premier performers to date have been two probes named *Voyager 1* and *Voyager 2*. Their travels to Jupiter, Saturn and beyond have dramatically broadened our knowledge of the giant gaseous planets. And in no other mission have computers played so significant a role.

The twin Voyagers left Earth in 1977 within 16 days of each other, when their destination planets were aligned in a way that would not recur for nearly two centuries. *Voyager 1* was to study Jupiter and Saturn; *Voyager 2* was to follow along on a slightly different trajectory as a backup. Each craft was packed with scientific instruments for investigating not only the planets and their rings and moons, but interplanetary space as well.

The Voyagers were set apart from earlier probes by the capabilities of their computers. Three different computer systems were put aboard each craft and given separate responsibility for guidance, data handling and overall command. Although the computers were designed to manage the probes handily on their own, they could also be reprogrammed from Earth to meet unanticipated needs.

This flexibility has yielded a particular bonanza of information from *Voyager 2*, featured on the following pages. Once *Voyager 1* successfully completed its tour of duty and headed out of the solar system, mission controllers reprogrammed *Voyager 2* for an extended flight plan that would carry it beyond Saturn and on to the unexplored realms of Uranus and Neptune. Since then, the probe's versatile computers have served with distinction, adapting to the challenge of data collection and transmissions at distances undreamed of when the craft was hurled skyward more than a decade ago.

A Long Leash for an Interplanetary Probe

As its identical twin did, *Voyager 2* operates much of the time without direct supervision from Earth. The spacecraft has a crew of on-board computers that take care of routine tasks automatically, keeping the craft properly oriented and monitoring equipment as part of their everyday chores *(pages 106-107)*. When certain emergencies arise — such as an equipment failure requiring an immediate switch to a backup — *Voyager 2* can take remedial action on its own. The craft relies on maintaining contact with home only to report its findings and to receive new instructions as the journey progresses.

Because the Voyager craft could not possibly store instructions for all the contingencies of its years-long mission, its computers are programmed to carry out various sets of commands, called sequences, that are transmitted, or uplinked, through a communications system known as the Deep Space Network *(below, right)*. Each sequence covers a period ranging in length from a day — during planetary encounters, when the scientific instruments are busily collecting data — to six months, when the probe is cruising between worlds. Once a sequence is received, the on-board computers execute it, handling all operations until the next sequence arrives. The computers maneuver the spacecraft by firing thrusters, turn scientific instruments on and off, and prepare data for transmission back to Earth.

Although limiting Voyager's independence, this arrangement allows researchers to respond readily to the probe's discoveries. With new sequences of commands, ground controllers can redirect experiments and, thanks to the computers' flexibility, reprogram the system to correct or circumvent malfunctions.

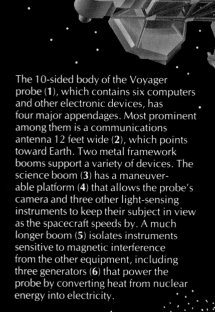

The 10-sided body of the Voyager probe (**1**), which contains six computers and other electronic devices, has four major appendages. Most prominent among them is a communications antenna 12 feet wide (**2**), which points toward Earth. Two metal framework booms support a variety of devices. The science boom (**3**) has a maneuverable platform (**4**) that allows the probe's camera and three other light-sensing instruments to keep their subject in view as the spacecraft speeds by. A much longer boom (**5**) isolates instruments sensitive to magnetic interference from the other equipment, including three generators (**6**) that power the probe by converting heat from nuclear energy into electricity.

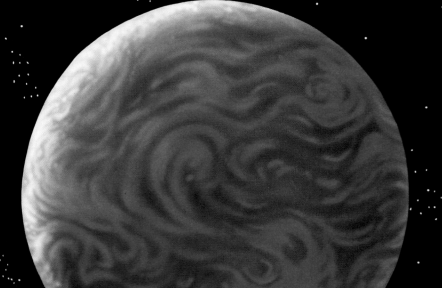

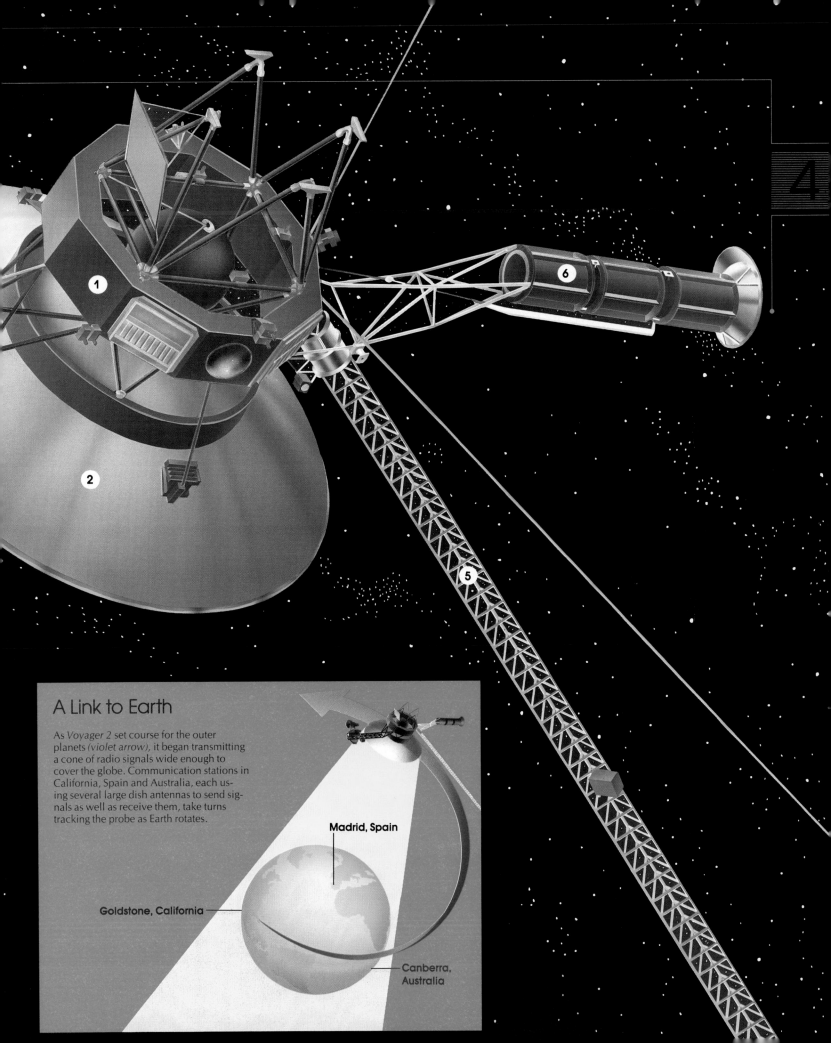

A Link to Earth

As *Voyager 2* set course for the outer planets *(violet arrow)*, it began transmitting a cone of radio signals wide enough to cover the globe. Communication stations in California, Spain and Australia, each using several large dish antennas to send signals as well as receive them, take turns tracking the probe as Earth rotates.

Madrid, Spain

Goldstone, California

Canberra, Australia

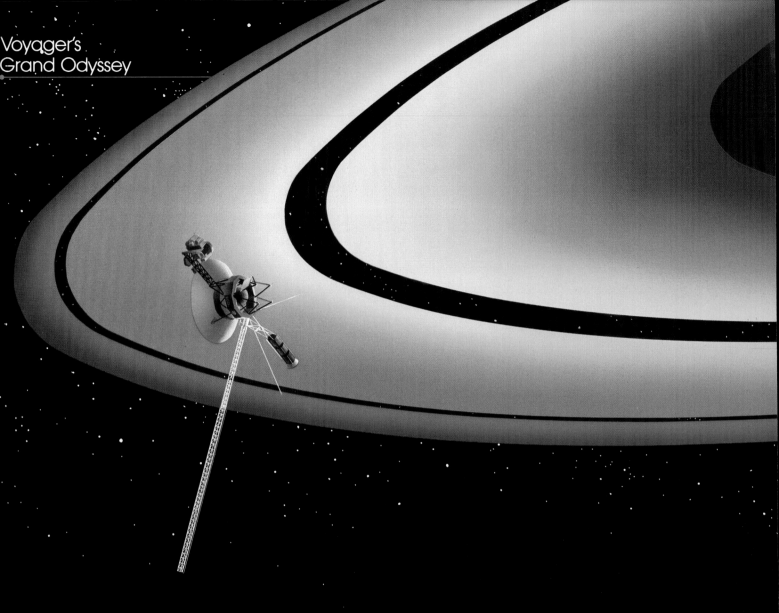

All Systems Go
at Saturn

Four years into its odyssey across the solar system, *Voyager 2* had left Jupiter behind and was approaching Saturn's spectacular rings *(above)*. By then, the probe's on-board computers had repeatedly demonstrated their ability to perform their missions. Of the six computers aboard, two share a supervisory role as commander, and two function as attitude-controllers, one to back up the other. Of the remaining two, one serves as a flight-data computer, managing data collection. The other serves as a backup, except during encounter with the planet, when it compresses image data for transmission *(pages 112-113)*.

The probe's designers assigned overall authority for the mission to the command computers, which receive the sequences of instructions uplinked from Earth and issue the appropriate orders to the other computers. In addition, they are ever alert to equipment malfunctions. For instance, the command computers have been programmed to expect a special six-bit code called the heartbeat from their subordinate, the attitude-control computer, almost every other second. Should the code not arrive, the command computers would engage the backup.

Attentive monitoring of the attitude-control computer is essential because of its role in maintaining communications with Earth. To keep the probe's antenna pointing earthward, this computer uses the positions of the sun and stars or, when celestial reference points are blocked by a planet or moon, data from internal gyros *(page 53)* to check the craft's orientation. Then it fires thrusters to make any adjustments. Upon receiving instructions from Earth, the attitude-control computer can move the science boom's platform to aim the probe's cameras and other light-sensing instruments, or even to alter the spacecraft's course toward a new destination.

The flight-data computer concentrates on *Voyager 2's* main purpose — gathering information and getting it safely back to Earth. This computer controls all 10 scientific instruments and prepares the results of their labor for transmission. In addition to scientific data, it collects and prepares engineering data — status reports on equipment performance — so that ground controllers, as well as the command computers, can keep a watchful eye on the craft.

The Flow of Commands and Data

Instructions from Earth arriving at *Voyager 2's* antenna *(yellow arrows)* follow a complex route as the probe's computers and other systems execute the commands and transmit responses to Earth *(green arrows)*. First, a modem converts analog signals into digital pulses for the command computers. These machines monitor the probe's health, operate a tape recorder to store data, and act as a clearinghouse for the flight-data and the attitude-control computers. The attitude-control computer operates the movable platform and keeps the spacecraft properly oriented, reporting its activities to the command computers and to the flight-data computer. Supplied with this information, the flight-data computer activates the probe's scientific instruments in response to orders sent by the command computers. The collected data is either stored temporarily on tape or forwarded to the spacecraft's antenna for transmission to Earth.

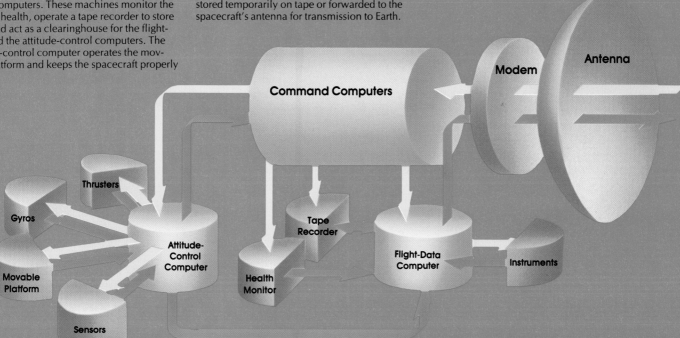

Instruments Aplenty for Studying Uranus

More than four years after leaving Saturn, *Voyager 2* was still able to apply its full data-collection capabilities for a look at Uranus, an enigmatic, ringed planet 1.7 billion miles from Earth. A flight-data computer brought instruments for 10 scientific experiments into play for two types of investigations: direct sensing of magnetic fields and particles encountered by the probe as it sped past the planet, and remote sensing of distant features, such as the planet's moons and atmosphere.

One mystery resolved by direct-sensing instruments was whether Uranus has a magnetic field. Instruments called magnetometers *(below)* detected magnetic forces around the planet, and a variety of particle detectors confirmed the presence of the field. Using these measurements, *Voyager* surveyed Uranus' magnetosphere — the region of charged particles trapped in space by a planet's magnetic field — to determine the strength of the field (comparable to Earth's) and its orientation.

Results from the remote sensors included stunning images *(pages 110-111)* taken by the probe's two cameras: Mounted on the movable platform, the telephoto and wide-angle cameras *(right)* could be pointed in specific directions. Three other light-sensing instruments on the platform uncovered details about the planet's satellites and the width and density of its rings, some so faint that astronomers had never detected them before. And by examining the composition of the atmosphere, remote sensors helped gauge the effects of Uranus' unique orientation — lying on its side, its axis of rotation pointed sunward during *Voyager 2's* visit.

Not missing a trick, *Voyager* even used its communications antenna as an investigating tool: Alterations in radio signals as the craft passed behind Uranus yielded still more data on the planet's atmosphere and the structure of its rings.

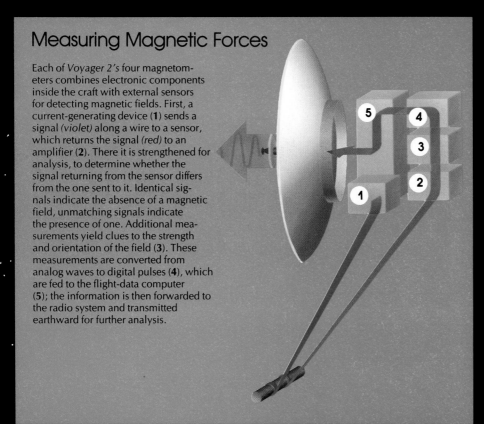

Measuring Magnetic Forces

Each of *Voyager 2's* four magnetometers combines electronic components inside the craft with external sensors for detecting magnetic fields. First, a current-generating device (**1**) sends a signal *(violet)* along a wire to a sensor, which returns the signal *(red)* to an amplifier (**2**). There it is strengthened for analysis, to determine whether the signal returning from the sensor differs from the one sent to it. Identical signals indicate the absence of a magnetic field, unmatching signals indicate the presence of one. Additional measurements yield clues to the strength and orientation of the field (**3**). These measurements are converted from analog waves to digital pulses (**4**), which are fed to the flight-data computer (**5**); the information is then forwarded to the radio system and transmitted earthward for further analysis.

Ten instruments aboard *Voyager 2* record a wide range of data about space. The imaging subsystem (**1**) includes a camera with a telephoto lens for close-ups and a camera with a wide-angle lens for global vistas. A photopolarimeter (**2**) studies atmospheres, rings and satellite surfaces by measuring how they reflect light. Two spectrometers (**3**) focus on special wavelengths of light: The infrared spectrometer gauges atmospheric composition and temperature, and the ultraviolet spectrometer examines auroras and other phenomena in the atmosphere. A plasma detector (**4**), a cosmic-ray detector (**5**) and a low-energy charged-particle detector (**6**) analyze charged particles that the probe encounters. High-field and low-field magnetometers (**7**) measure strong and weak magnetic fields respectively; the low-field sensors, on the magnetometer boom, stay clear of magnetic interference from the probe itself. Plasma-wave and radio-astronomy experiments share two long antennas (**8**) to detect radio signals emitted by charged particles trapped in the radiation belts of celestial bodies.

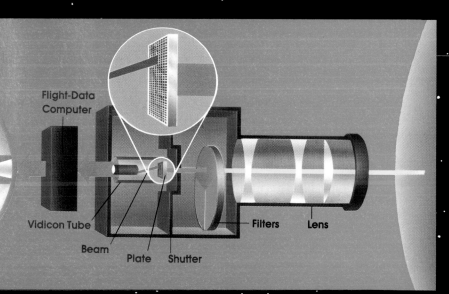

Taking Photos in Space

To show details visible only in some wavelengths of light, cameras record separate images through various colored filters. Here, light passes through a lens, a blue filter and a shutter, then strikes an electrically charged plate at one end of a vidicon tube, causing an electron image to form on the back of the plate. Electrons will be present in dark areas, absent in light areas. From the other end, an electron beam scans the plate, replacing lost electrons in proportion to the intensity of light *(inset)*. A brightness value is assigned to each picture element on the plate and sent via the flight-data computer to Earth.

Flight-Data Computer

Vidicon Tube

Beam

Plate

Shutter

Filters

Lens

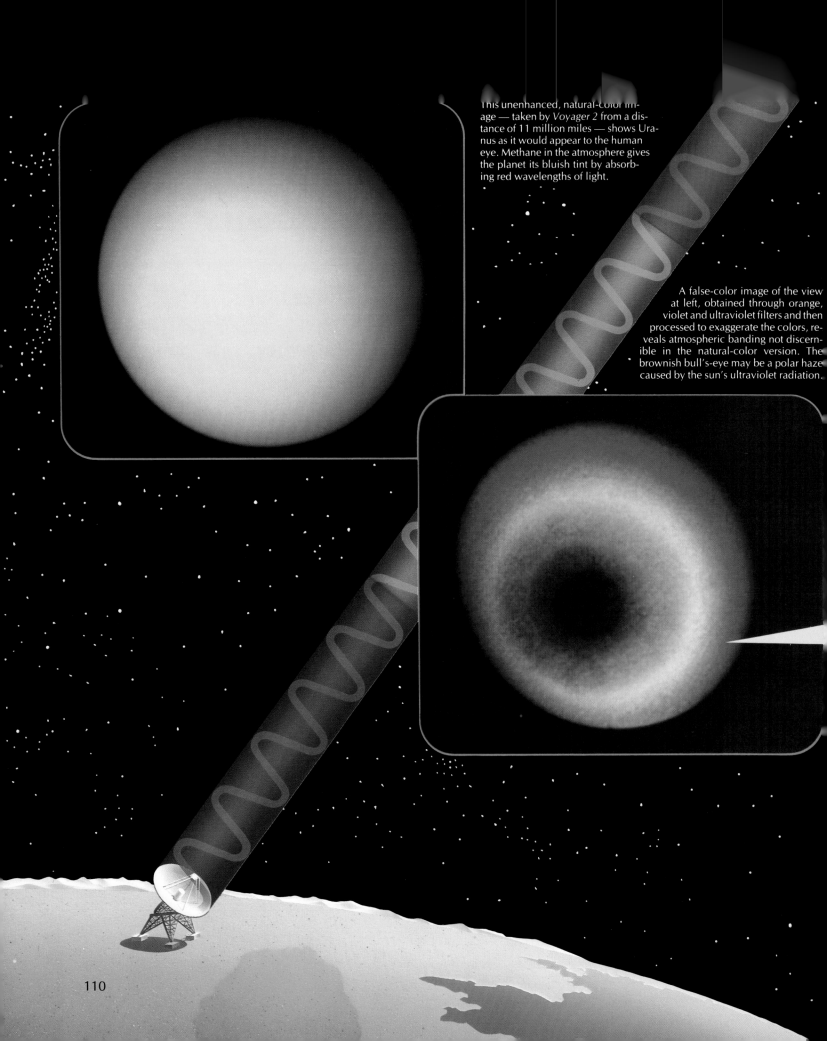

This unenhanced, natural-color image — taken by *Voyager 2* from a distance of 11 million miles — shows Uranus as it would appear to the human eye. Methane in the atmosphere gives the planet its bluish tint by absorbing red wavelengths of light.

A false-color image of the view at left, obtained through orange, violet and ultraviolet filters and then processed to exaggerate the colors, reveals atmospheric banding not discernible in the natural-color version. The brownish bull's-eye may be a polar haze caused by the sun's ultraviolet radiation.

Turning Raw Data into Detail-Rich Images

Data collected by *Voyager 2's* flight-data computer, having been beamed back to a station of the Deep Space Network, is forwarded to the mission's ground computers at the Jet Propulsion Laboratory (JPL) in Pasadena, California. These machines, which process all of *Voyager's* data, are best known for the black-and-white and color pictures they construct from the millions of ones and zeros that constitute the probe's imaging data.

To produce a color image, JPL computers combine images taken through blue, green and orange filters. Values that were measured through each filter now light up one of the three phosphors — red, green and blue — that make up each picture element, or pixel, of a computer's color monitor. (The probe's cameras are insensitive to red light, hence their use of an orange filter.) The human eye blends these colors into a variety of hues that depend on the brightness of each phosphor. Although the image gains natural color *(far left)*, it may show little detail. Two color techniques are commonly used to uncover features that the human eye would miss. In one, values produced by other filters — the cameras have several, including ultraviolet and violet ones — are then assigned to the red, green and blue phosphors to create a false-color image that reveals hidden detail.

In the other technique, mission scientists call upon the JPL computers to manipulate image data, exaggerating the slightest variations in color and contrast so that humans can appreciate them *(left)*. Such image-processing techniques, known as color enhancement *(below)* and contrast enhancement *(bottom)*, help make visible the full richness of visual information captured during the fly-by.

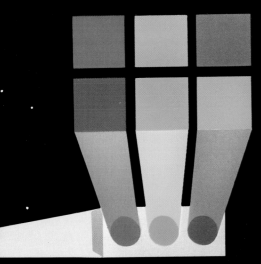

To create the enhanced, false-color picture of Uranus on the opposite page, operators at JPL first assigned, pixel by pixel, the image taken through the orange filter aboard *Voyager 2* to the red phosphors of the computer monitor, the violet-filter image to the green phosphors and the ultraviolet-filter image to the blue phosphors. The resulting hues, shown in the top row of boxes *(left)*, produced a picture having color variations that were subtle and hard to detect. To delineate the banding more clearly, a computer exaggerated the ratio of red to green and of blue to green for each pixel, producing deeper reds and brighter blues, as shown in the lower row of boxes.

Contrast Enhancement to Bring Out Detail

An unenhanced black-and-white image of Uranus' moon Titania *(below, left)* reveals few details of the satellite's surface because most of the pixels lie within a small portion of the range of black-to-white tones known as the gray scale. But this portion can be stretched. The computer divides the gray scale into 256 steps, numbered 0 to 255. (The human eye can distinguish only 25 steps between black and white.) By redistributing the original image's small range of tones — in this case they all lie between tone 129 and tone 167 — over the entire gray scale *(below, center)*, an image-processing computer enhances the contrast, revealing more detail *(below, right)*.

0   129 167   255

The Challenges of Darkness and Distance

Two difficulties confronted *Voyager* at Uranus. Dim sunlight lengthened exposures, raising the risk of blurred images. In addition, transmissions from the probe, weak from traveling twice the distance between Saturn and Earth, were likely to fade into the background radio noise of space.

To get sharp pictures, cameras had to track their targets as the probe sped by Uranus at more than 40,000 miles per hour. The camera platform on *Voyager's* science boom could not do so on its own; the entire spacecraft had to turn. Because the attitude-control computer would reject maneuvers that aimed the antenna away from Earth, controllers temporarily simulated a drift. When the computer fired thrusters to compensate, it provided the required panning motion. Then, to keep the cameras as steady as possible, engineers fine-tuned the computer's control of spacecraft wobble *(below, right)*.

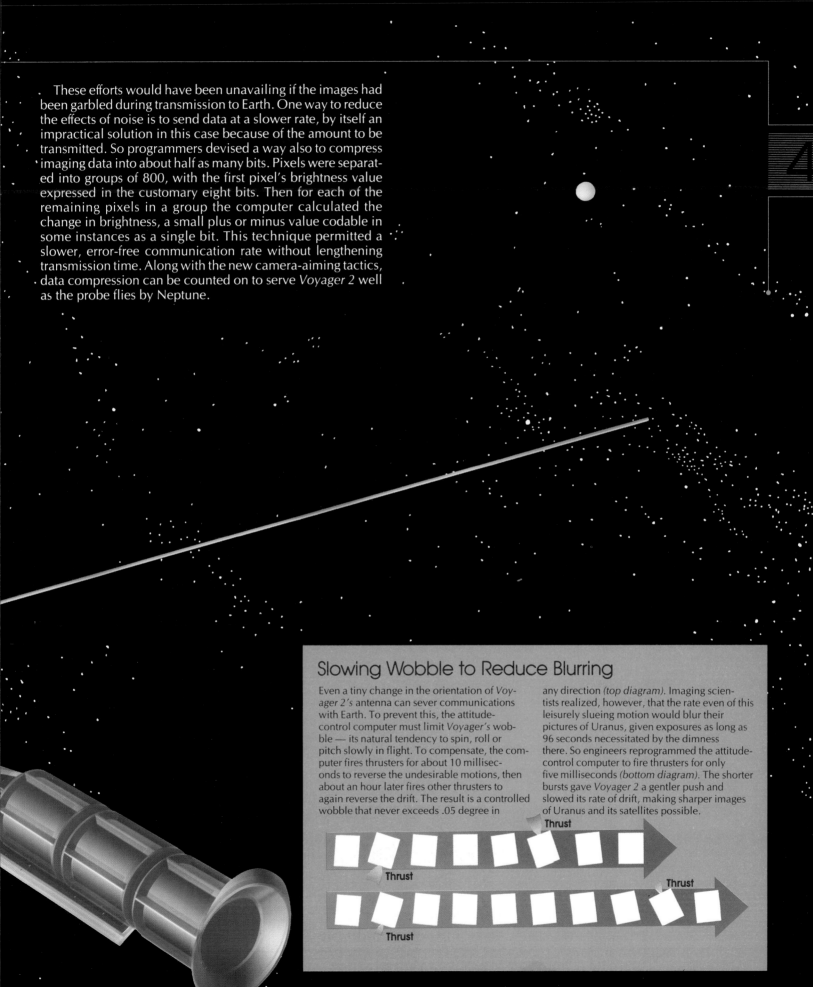

These efforts would have been unavailing if the images had been garbled during transmission to Earth. One way to reduce the effects of noise is to send data at a slower rate, by itself an impractical solution in this case because of the amount to be transmitted. So programmers devised a way also to compress imaging data into about half as many bits. Pixels were separated into groups of 800, with the first pixel's brightness value expressed in the customary eight bits. Then for each of the remaining pixels in a group the computer calculated the change in brightness, a small plus or minus value codable in some instances as a single bit. This technique permitted a slower, error-free communication rate without lengthening transmission time. Along with the new camera-aiming tactics, data compression can be counted on to serve *Voyager 2* well as the probe flies by Neptune.

Slowing Wobble to Reduce Blurring

Even a tiny change in the orientation of *Voyager 2's* antenna can sever communications with Earth. To prevent this, the attitude-control computer must limit *Voyager's* wobble — its natural tendency to spin, roll or pitch slowly in flight. To compensate, the computer fires thrusters for about 10 milliseconds to reverse the undesirable motions, then about an hour later fires other thrusters to again reverse the drift. The result is a controlled wobble that never exceeds .05 degree in any direction *(top diagram)*. Imaging scientists realized, however, that the rate even of this leisurely slueing motion would blur their pictures of Uranus, given exposures as long as 96 seconds necessitated by the dimness there. So engineers reprogrammed the attitude-control computer to fire thrusters for only five milliseconds *(bottom diagram)*. The shorter bursts gave *Voyager 2* a gentler push and slowed its rate of drift, making sharper images of Uranus and its satellites possible.

Thrust

Thrust

Thrust

Thrust

Where Probes Have Gone

Since October 1957, when the Soviet satellite *Sputnik I* announced the dawn of the space age, more than 3,500 payloads have been successfully rocketed beyond Earth's atmosphere. By far most have been military, commercial and scientific satellites that travel in Earth orbit. Manned spacecraft, which make up slightly more than three percent of the total, have ventured only as far as the moon. Thus it has been left to an even smaller number of robotic explorers to take on more distant surveillance of the solar system. The missions of the unmanned probes — for the most part sent aloft by either

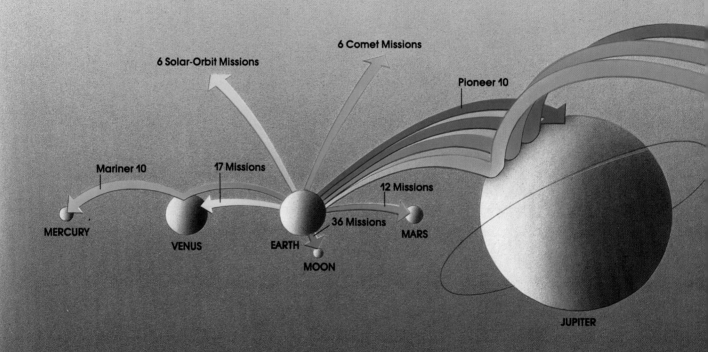

6 Comet Missions

6 Solar-Orbit Missions

Pioneer 10

Mariner 10

17 Missions

12 Missions

36 Missions

MERCURY

VENUS

EARTH

MOON

MARS

JUPITER

the United States or the Soviet Union—are represented as colored arrows on the schematic planetary chart below.

During the early years of space flight, Earth's moon was the most popular target: Between 1959 and 1976, thirty-six lunar probes *(red)* made the quarter-million-mile trip. Six probes *(mustard)* were sent into orbit around the sun between 1965 and 1976; six others were dispatched to observe various comets *(orange)* from 1978 to 1985.

In 1962, *Mariner 2* led the way to the planets with a flight past Venus, the first of 17 successful missions *(yellow)* from Earth to its nearest planetary neighbor. A succession of 12 flights to Mars *(bright orange)* began in 1964 with the launch of *Mariner 4*. Eight years later, in 1972, *Pioneer 10* left Earth to become the first craft to fly by Jupiter *(purple)*.

The remaining five planets have been targeted by multi-mission probes: *Mariner 10*, sent in 1973 to Venus and then on to Mercury *(light green)*, *Pioneer 11 (green)* to Jupiter and Saturn in 1973, followed by *Voyager 1 (aqua)* in 1977. Launched the same year, *Voyager 2 (blue)* continued past Saturn on the way to Uranus and Neptune.

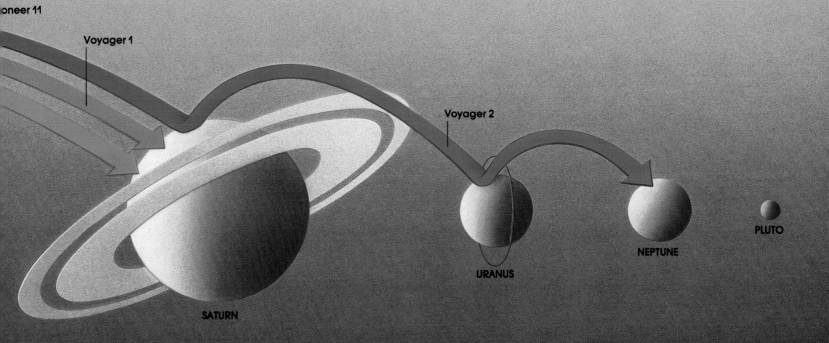

Pioneer 11

Voyager 1

Voyager 2

SATURN

URANUS

NEPTUNE

PLUTO

Highlights of Space Achievements

Since the dawn of space flight in 1957, thousands of craft have been sent beyond Earth's atmosphere to perform a vast variety of tasks. This chronology spotlights the manned space effort and the programs to propel unmanned probes deeper into the cosmos.

1957
OCT. 4 — *SPUTNIK I (USSR)* First man-made Earth satellite.

NOV. 3 — *SPUTNIK II (USSR)* First satellite to collect biological data from orbit; carried dog Laika.

1958
JAN. 31 — *EXPLORER I (USA)* First American Earth satellite.

MAR. 17 — *VANGUARD (USA)* First satellite to use solar power.

MAY 15 — *SPUTNIK III (USSR)* First comprehensive geophysical data from orbit.

1959
JAN. 2 — *LUNA 1 (USSR)* First spacecraft to achieve Earth-escape velocity; missed the moon and went into orbit around the sun.

MAR. 3 — *PIONEER 4 (USA)* First deep-space probe; passed within 37,300 miles of the moon.

MAY 28 — *JUPITER (USA)* First primates in space (Able and Baker); suborbital.

SEPT. 12 — *LUNA 2 (USSR)* First lunar probe to impact on moon; no data returned.

OCT. 4 — *LUNA 3 (USSR)* First lunar probe to photograph the moon's far side.

1960
AUG. 19 — *SPUTNIK V (USSR)* First retrieval of orbited animals (dogs Strelka and Belka).

1961
JAN. 31 — *MERCURY-REDSTONE 2 (USA)* First test of Mercury-Redstone with passenger aboard (chimpanzee Ham); suborbital.

FEB. 12 — *VENERA 1 (USSR)* Venus probe; passed within 62,000 miles of Venus.

APR. 12 — *VOSTOK 1 (USSR)* First manned space flight; Yuri Gagarin; one orbit; 1 hour 48 minutes.

MAY 5 — *MERCURY-REDSTONE 3 (USA)* First American manned suborbital flight; Alan Shepard; 15 minutes 22 seconds.

JULY 21 — *MERCURY-REDSTONE 4 (USA)* Manned suborbital flight; Gus Grissom; 15 minutes 37 seconds.

AUG. 6 — *VOSTOK 2 (USSR)* Manned orbital space flight; Gherman Titov; 16 orbits; 25 hours.

1962
FEB. 20 — *MERCURY-ATLAS 6 (USA)* First American manned orbital flight; John Glenn; three orbits; 4 hours 54 minutes.

APR. 23 — *RANGER 4 (USA)* First American lunar probe to impact on moon; equipment failed; no pictures returned.

MAY 24 — *MERCURY-ATLAS 7 (USA)* Manned mission; Scott Carpenter; three orbits; 4 hours 54 minutes.

AUG. 11 — *VOSTOK 3 (USSR)* Part of first Soviet dual mission (with *Vostok 4*); A. Nikolayev; 64 orbits; 3 days 22 hours.

AUG. 12 — *VOSTOK 4 (USSR)* Part of the first Soviet dual mission (with *Vostok 3*); came within 3.1 miles of *Vostok 3* on the first orbit; P. Popovich; 48 orbits; 2 days 23 hours.

AUG. 27 — *MARINER 2 (USA)* First successful fly-by of Venus.

OCT. 3 — *MERCURY-ATLAS 8 (USA)* Manned mission; Walter Schirra; six orbits; 9 hours.

1963
MAY 15 — *MERCURY-ATLAS 9 (USA)* First American manned flight to exceed 24 hours; Gordon Cooper; 22 orbits; 34 hours 20 minutes.

JUNE 14 — *VOSTOK 5 (USSR)* Part of dual mission (with *Vostok 6*); V. Bykovsky; 81 orbits; 5 days 23 hours.

JUNE 16 — *VOSTOK 6 (USSR)* Dual mission (with *Vostok 5*); came within 3 miles of *Vostok 5*; Valentina Tereshkova (first woman in space); 48 orbits; 2 days 22 hours 48 minutes.

1964
JULY 28 — *RANGER 7 (USA)* First successful American lunar probe; impacted on moon; returned 4,316 close-up photos of lunar surface down to impact.

OCT. 12 — *VOSKHOD I (USSR)* First three-man orbital mission; V. Kamarov, K. Feoktistov, B. Yegerav; 16 orbits; 24 hours 18 minutes.

NOV. 28 — *MARINER 4 (USA)* First successful fly-by of Mars.

1965
MAR. 18 — *VOSKHOD II (USSR)* First space walk; A. Leonov (performed 10-minute extravehicular activity, or EVA), P. Belyayev; 17 orbits; 26 hours.

MAR. 23 — *GEMINI 3 (USA)* First American two-man crew; first manned orbital maneuvers; Gus Grissom, John Young; three orbits; 4 hours 54 minutes.

JUNE 3 — *GEMINI 4 (USA)* First American space walk; Edward White (performed 21-minute EVA); James McDivitt; 62 orbits; 4 days 1 hour.

AUG. 21 — *GEMINI 5 (USA)* The first extended manned flight; Gordon Cooper, Charles Conrad; 128 orbits; 7 days 22 hours.

DEC. 4 — *GEMINI 7 (USA)* First rendezvous in space (with *Gemini 6*); Frank Borman, James Lovell; 220 orbits; 13 days 18 hours 35 minutes.

DEC. 15 — *GEMINI 6 (USA)* First rendezvous in space (with *Gemini 7*); Walter Schirra, Thomas Stafford; 16 orbits; 25 hours 51 minutes.

1966

JAN. 31 — *LUNA 9 (USSR)* First soft landing on moon; returned lunar-surface photos.

MAR. 16 — *GEMINI 8 (USA)* First docking in space with previously launched target *(Agena 8)*; malfunction caused mission to be curtailed; Neil Armstrong, David Scott; 10 hours 41 minutes.

MAR. 31 — *LUNA 10 (USSR)* First lunar orbiter; returned lunar data until May 1966.

MAY 30 — *SURVEYOR 1 (USA)* First American soft landing on moon; returned 11,240 photographs.

JUNE 3 — *GEMINI 9 (USA)* Rendezvoused with Agena target; 2-hour-8-minute EVA carried out; Thomas Stafford, Eugene Cernan; 3 days.

JULY 18 — *GEMINI 10 (USA)* First use of target vehicle as source of propulsion after rendezvous and docking; first double rendezvous (with *Agena 10* and *Agena 8)*; first retrieval of space object (test package on target vehicle) during space walk; John Young, Michael Collins; 2 days 22 hours 48 minutes.

AUG. 10 — *LUNAR ORBITER 1 (USA)* Orbited moon and returned 207 photos of lunar equatorial region as part of program to aid selection of landing sites for later missions; all orbiters were deliberately crashed on the moon so that their radio transmitters would not interfere with later spacecraft.

SEPT. 12 — *GEMINI 11 (USA)* Rendezvous and docking achieved on first revolution; used *Agena 11* propulsion to achieve record altitude of 850 miles; Charles Conrad, Richard Gordon; 2 days 23 hours.

NOV. 11 — *GEMINI 12 (USA)* Final Gemini mission; three EVAs, for record total of 5 hours 30 minutes; James Lovell, Buzz Aldrin; 3 days 22 hours.

1967

JAN. 27 — *APOLLO 1 (USA)* Fire inside spacecraft during ground testing resulted in death of three astronauts; Gus Grissom, Edward White, Roger Chaffee.

APR. 23 — *SOYUZ 1 (USSR)* First manned test flight of the new Soyuz spacecraft; V. Komarov killed on ground impact when parachute lines of the reentry module were fouled.

JUNE 12 — *VENERA 4 (USSR)* First successful probe of atmosphere on planet Venus.

AUG. 1 — *LUNAR ORBITER 5 (USA)* Photographed five potential Apollo landing sites; ended lunar orbiter mapping program.

1968

SEPT. 15 — *ZOND 5 (USSR)* First circumlunar flight to return to Earth; carried live organisms; recovered in Indian Ocean.

OCT. 11 — *APOLLO 7 (USA)* First American three-man Earth-orbital mission; Wally Schirra, Donn Eisele, Walt Cunningham; 10 days 20 hours.

OCT. 25 — *SOYUZ 2 (USSR)* Unmanned satellite; rendezvous target for *Soyuz 3.*

OCT. 26 — *SOYUZ 3 (USSR)* Manned spacecraft; maneuvered to within 650 feet of *Soyuz 2;* G. Beregovoi; 3 days 22 hours 54 minutes.

DEC. 21 — *APOLLO 8 (USA)* First manned orbit of moon; Frank Borman, James Lovell, William Anders; 10 lunar orbits; 6 days 3 hours in space overall.

1969

JAN. 14 — *SOYUZ 4 (USSR)* First docking (with *Soyuz 5)* of two manned Soviet spacecraft; V. Shatalov; 2 days 23 hours.

JAN. 15 — *SOYUZ 5 (USSR)* Docked with *Soyuz 4;* B. Volyanov, A. Yeliseyev, Y. Khronov; 3 days.

MAR. 3 — *APOLLO 9 (USA)* First test of lunar module in Earth orbit; James McDivitt, David Scott, Russell Schweickart; 10 days 1 hour.

MAY 18 — *APOLLO 10 (USA)* First test of lunar module in lunar orbit; Thomas Stafford, Eugene Cernan, John Young; 31 lunar orbits; 8 days in space overall.

JULY 16 — *APOLLO 11 (USA)* First manned lunar landing; first men to walk on moon's surface; Neil Armstrong, Buzz Aldrin, Michael Collins; 22 hours on moon, with 2 hours 35 minutes of EVA.

OCT. 11 — *SOYUZ 6 (USSR)* First triple launch (with *Soyuz 7* and *8)* of manned craft; nondocking group flight; G. Shonin, N. Kubasov; 4 days 22 hours.

OCT. 12 — *SOYUZ 7 (USSR)* Target vehicle for group rendezvous (with *Soyuz 6* and *8);* A. Filipchenko, V. Volkov, V. Gorbatko; 4 days 22 hours.

OCT. 13 — *SOYUZ 8 (USSR)* Flagship in maneuvers (with *Soyuz 6* and *7);* V. Shatalov, A. Yeliseyev; 4 days 22 hours.

NOV. 14 — *APOLLO 12 (USA)* Second manned lunar landing; returned parts from *Surveyor 3;* Pete Conrad, Richard Gordon, Alan Bean; 32 hours on moon, with 7 hours 45 minutes of EVA.

1970

APR. 11 — *APOLLO 13 (USA)* Third manned lunar-landing attempt, aborted due to oxygen-tank explosion in service module; crew returned safely; James Lovell, Fred Haise, Jack Swigert; 5 days 22 hours.

JUNE 2 — *SOYUZ 9 (USSR)* Set new duration record for manned space flight; V. Sevastianov, A. Nikolayev; 17 days 16 hours.

AUG. 17 — *VENERA 7 (USSR)* Venus atmosphere probe; first successful landing on surface.

1971

JAN. 31 — *APOLLO 14 (USA)* Third manned lunar landing; collected 96 pounds of lunar samples; Alan Shepard, Stuart Roosa, Edgar Mitchell; 34 hours on moon, with 9 hours 24 minutes of EVA.

APR. 19 — *SALYUT 1 (USSR)* Unmanned prototype for orbiting space station and laboratory; decayed October 11, 1971.

APR. 23 — *SOYUZ 10 (USSR)* First crew to dock with orbiting *Salyut 1* (5 hours 30 minutes); V. Shatalov, A. Yeliseyev, N. Rukavishnikov.

MAY 30 — *MARINER 9 (USA)* First successful Mars orbiter; returned 7,000 pictures of surface and moons.

JUNE 6 — *SOYUZ 11 (USSR)* First crew to occupy orbiting Salyut space station (22 days); because of accidental depressurization, cosmonauts died on reentry; G. Dobrovolsky, V. Volkov, V. Patsayev.

JULY 26 — *APOLLO 15 (USA)* Fourth manned lunar landing; first use of manned Lunar Roving Vehicle; David Scott, Alfred Worden, James Irwin; 67 hours on moon, with 18 hours 35 minutes of EVA.

1972
MAR. 2 — *PIONEER 10 (USA)* First successful fly-by of Jupiter (December 1973); first probe to escape solar system (June 1983).

APR. 16 — *APOLLO 16 (USA)* Fifth manned lunar landing; collected 213 pounds of lunar samples; Charles Duke, Ken Mattingly, John Young; 71 hours on moon, with 20 hours 15 minutes of EVA.

DEC. 7 — *APOLLO 17 (USA)* Sixth and last Apollo manned lunar landing; collected 243 pounds of lunar samples; Eugene Cernan, Ronald Evans, Harrison Schmitt; record 76 hours on moon, with a total of 23 hours 12 minutes of EVA.

1973
APR. 5 — *PIONEER 11 (USA)* Jupiter probe; first successful fly-by of Saturn (September 1979).

MAY 14 — *SKYLAB (USA)* First unmanned American space station; placed in Earth orbit but damaged during launch.

MAY 25 — *SKYLAB 1 (USA)* First crew to occupy Skylab (28 days); replaced thermal shield and repaired solar wing; Pete Conrad, Joseph Kerwin, Paul Weitz.

JULY 28 — *SKYLAB 2 (USA)* Second crew to occupy Skylab (59 days); Alan Bean, Jack Lousma, Owen Barriott.

SEPT. 27 — *SOYUZ 12 (USSR)* Test of modified spacecraft (chemical batteries replace extensible solar panels) for ferry missions to orbiting Salyut laboratories; V. Lazarev, O. Makarov.

NOV. 3 — *MARINER 10 (USA)* First craft to use gravity of one planet (Venus) to reach another (Mercury); first television pictures of Mercury.

NOV. 16 — *SKYLAB 3 (USA)* Third and last crew to occupy Skylab; longest Skylab mission (84 days); Gerald Carr, Edward Gibson, William Pogue.

DEC. 18 — *SOYUZ 13 (USSR)* Manned spacecraft; astrophysical, biological and Earth-resources experiments; P. Klimuk, V. Lebedev; 7 days 20 hours 55 minutes.

1974
JUNE 24 — *SALYUT 3 (USSR)* Unmanned space station; in orbit 214 days.

JULY 3 — *SOYUZ 14 (USSR)* Manned spacecraft; crew rendezvoused and docked with *Salyut 3* (14.5 days); P. Popovich, Y. Artyukhin.

AUG. 26 — *SOYUZ 15 (USSR)* Manned spacecraft; failed to dock with *Salyut 3*; G. Sarafanov, L. Demir.

DEC. 2 — *SOYUZ 16 (USSR)* Manned spacecraft; tested new design for joint US-USSR Apollo-Soyuz Test Project; A. Filipchenko, N. Rukavishnikov.

DEC. 26 — *SALYUT 4 (USSR)* Unmanned space station; in orbit 770 days.

1975
JAN. 11 — *SOYUZ 17 (USSR)* Manned spacecraft; crew docked with and occupied *Salyut 4* (28 days); A. Gubarev, G. Grechko.

MAY 24 — *SOYUZ 18 (USSR)* Second crew to occupy *Salyut 4* (63 days); P. Klimuk, V. Sevastyanov.

JUNE 8 — *VENERA 9 (USSR)* Venus probe; soft-landed and returned first TV pictures from surface.

JULY 15 — *APOLLO-SOYUZ (USA-USSR)* First cooperative international flight; docked in Earth orbit for two days; T. Stafford, V. Brand, D. Slayton (USA); A. Leonov, V. Kubasov (USSR).

AUG. 20 — *VIKING 1 (USA)* Mars orbiter; first successful Mars landing; returned photographs and data.

SEPT. 9 — *VIKING 2 (USA)* Mars orbiter; landed; returned pictures and data.

NOV. 17 — *SOYUZ 20 (USSR)* Unmanned spacecraft; ground-controlled docking with *Salyut 4* in rehearsal for space-station resupply.

1976
JUNE 22 — *SALYUT 5 (USSR)* Unmanned space station; in orbit 412 days.

JULY 6 — *SOYUZ 21 (USSR)* Manned spacecraft; docked with *Salyut 5*; crew performed extensive experiments; B. Volynov, V. Zholobov; 49 days 6 hours.

SEPT. 15 — *SOYUZ 22 (USSR)* Manned spacecraft; carried multispectral camera; V. Bykovsky, V. Aksyonov; 7 days 21 hours 54 minutes.

OCT. 14 — *SOYUZ 23 (USSR)* Manned spacecraft; failed to dock with *Salyut 5*; V. Zudov, V. Rozhdestvensky.

1977
FEB. 7 — *SOYUZ 24 (USSR)* Manned spacecraft; docked with *Salyut 5*; tested and repaired parts aboard space station; V. Gorbatko, Y. Glazkov; 17 days 16 hours.

AUG. 20 — *VOYAGER 2 (USA)* Fly-by probe of Jupiter, Saturn, Uranus, Neptune; returned pictures and data over the course of 12 years.

SEPT. 5 — *VOYAGER 1 (USA)* Fly-by probe of Jupiter and Saturn; returned pictures and data on Jupiter and five of its moons and on Saturn and four of its moons.

SEPT. 29 — *SALYUT 6 (USSR)* Unmanned space station; sent into Earth orbit.

OCT. 9 — *SOYUZ 25 (USSR)* Manned spacecraft; failed to dock with *Salyut 6*; V. Kovalenok, V. Ryumin.

DEC. 10 — *SOYUZ 26 (USSR)* Manned spacecraft; docked with *Salyut 6*; 1 hour 28 minutes of extravehicular activity; Y. Romanenko, G. Grechko; 96 days 10 hours.

1978

JAN. 10 — *SOYUZ 27 (USSR)* Manned spacecraft; docked with *Salyut 6*, achieving first three-spacecraft complex (with *Soyuz 26)*; V. Dzhanibekov, O. Makarov; 6 days.

JAN. 20 — *PROGRESS 1 (USSR)* Unmanned, expendable transport craft to resupply *Salyut 6* with propellants, food and other cargo; on February 7 it was made to reenter the atmosphere and burn up.

MAR. 2 — *SOYUZ 28 (USSR)* Manned spacecraft; docked with *Salyut 6*; first international crew to occupy *Salyut 6*; A. Gubarev, V. Remek (Czechoslovakia); 7 days 20 hours.

JUNE 15 — *SOYUZ 29 (USSR)* Manned spacecraft; docked with *Salyut 6*; performed 2-hour EVA to replace equipment and retrieve package exposed to space for 10 months; V. Kovalenok, A. Ivanchenkov; 139 days.

JUNE 27 — *SOYUZ 30 (USSR)* Manned spacecraft; international crew; docked with *Salyut 6*; performed biomedical experiments; P. Klimuk, M. Hermaszewski (Poland); 7 days 22 hours.

AUG. 8 — *PIONEER-VENUS 2 (USA)* Five entry probes measure Venus' atmosphere before landing; returned surface data.

AUG. 26 — *SOYUZ 31 (USSR)* Manned spacecraft; international crew; docked with *Salyut 6*; V. Bykovsky, S. Jaehn (East Germany); 7 days 20 hours.

1979

FEB. 25 — *SOYUZ 32 (USSR)* Seventh crew to occupy *Salyut 6*; deployed radio telescope; V. Lyakhov, V. Ryumin; 175 days.

APR. 10 — *SOYUZ 33 (USSR)* Manned spacecraft; failed to dock with *Salyut 6*; N. Rukavishnikov, G. Ivanov.

JUNE 6 — *SOYUZ 34 (USSR)* Unmanned spacecraft; ground-controlled docking with *Salyut 6* and *Soyuz 32*; returned on August 19 with crew from *Soyuz 32*.

DEC. 16 — *SOYUZ T-1 (USSR)* Unmanned, new-generation Soyuz spacecraft; ground-controlled docking with *Salyut 6*.

1980

APR. 9 — *SOYUZ 35 (USSR)* Manned spacecraft; eighth crew to occupy *Salyut 6*; L. Popov, V. Ryumin; 184 days 20 hours.

MAY 26 — *SOYUZ 36 (USSR)* Manned spacecraft; international crew; docked with *Salyut 6*; V. Kubasov, B. Farkas (Hungary); 7 days 20 hours.

JUNE 5 — *SOYUZ T-2 (USSR)* First manned flight of the Soyuz T series; docked with *Salyut 6*; Y. Malyshev, V. Aksyonov; 3 days 22 hours.

JULY 23 — *SOYUZ 37 (USSR)* Manned spacecraft; international crew; docked with *Salyut 6*; performed a series of experiments with resident crew (Popov and Ryumin); V. Gorbatko, P. Tuan (Vietnam); 7 days 20 hours.

SEPT. 18 — *SOYUZ 38 (USSR)* Manned spacecraft; international crew; ferried fuel and supplies to *Salyut 6*, and returned *Soyuz 35* crew; Y. Romanenko, A. Mendez (Cuba); 7 days 20 hours.

NOV. 27 — *SOYUZ T-3 (USSR)* Manned spacecraft; first Soyuz in nine years to carry three crew members; L. Kizim, G. Strelalov, O. Makarov; 15 days.

1981

MAR. 12 — *SOYUZ T-4 (USSR)* Manned spacecraft; docked with *Salyut 6*; carried out repairs to space station; V. Kovalenok, V. Savinykh; 76 days.

MAR. 22 — *SOYUZ 39 (USSR)* Manned spacecraft; international crew; docked with

Salyut 6; first TV transmission from space of holographic images; V. Dzhanibekov, J. Gurragcha (Mongolia); 9 days.

APRIL 12 — *STS-1 (USA)* First orbital test flight of space shuttle *Columbia*; tested cargo-bay doors; John Young, Robert Crippen; 2 days 6 hours.

MAY 14 — *SOYUZ 40 (USSR)* Manned spacecraft; international crew; docked with *Salyut 6*; studied effects of space on construction materials; L. Popov, D. Prunariu (Rumania); 9 days.

NOV. 12 — *STS-2 (USA)* Second orbital test flight of space shuttle *Columbia*; first in-flight test of manipulator arm; Joseph Engle, Richard Truly; 2 days 6 hours.

1982

MAR. 22 — *STS-3 (USA)* Third orbital test flight of space shuttle *Columbia*; first manipulation of payload in cargo bay; Jack Lousma, Gordon Fullerton; 8 days 4 hours.

APR. 19 — *SALYUT 7 (USSR)* Unmanned space station; test of systems and equipment for future crew occupation.

MAY 13 — *SOYUZ T-5 (USSR)* Manned spacecraft; docked with *Salyut 7*; A. Berezovoy, V. Lebedev; 211 days 9 hours.

JUNE 24 — *SOYUZ T-6 (USSR)* Manned spacecraft; international crew; docked with *Salyut 7*; V. Dzhanibekov, A. Ivanchenkov, J. Chretien (France); 7 days 21 hours.

JUNE 27 — *STS-4 (USA)* Fourth orbital test of space shuttle *Columbia*; first commercial experiments and scientific "getaway specials"; Ken Mattingly, Henry Hartsfield; 7 days 1 hour.

AUG. 19 — *SOYUZ T-7 (USSR)* Manned spacecraft; first coed crew (2 male, 1 female); docked with *Salyut 7*; L. Popov, A. Serebov, S. Savitskaya; 7 days 21 hours 52 minutes.

NOV. 11 — *STS-5 (USA)* Fifth flight of space shuttle *Columbia*; first operational manned shuttle flight; launched a pair of commercial satellites; Vance Brand, Robert Overmyer, William Lenoir, Joseph Allen; 5 days 2 hours.

1983

APR. 4 — *STS-6 (USA)* First flight of space shuttle *Challenger,* second shuttle in U.S. fleet; deployed tracking and data-relay satellite; Paul Weitz, Karol Bobko, F. Story Musgrave, Donald Peterson; 5 days 24 minutes.

APR. 20 — *SOYUZ T-8 (USSR)* Manned spacecraft; failed to dock with *Salyut 7;* V. Titov, G. Strekalov, A. Serebrov; 2 days 18 minutes.

JUNE 2 — *VENERA 15 (USSR)* Venus orbiter; entered 24-hour orbit of the planet on October 10, 1983; mapped the surface and carried out atmospheric research.

JUNE 7 — *VENERA 16 (USSR)* Venus orbiter; entered 24-hour orbit of the planet on October 14, 1983; mapped the surface and carried out atmospheric research.

JUNE 18 — *STS-7 (USA)* Second orbital test flight of space shuttle *Challenger:* deployed remote manipulator arm to retrieve a target satellite; Robert Crippen, Sally Ride (first U.S. woman in space), Norman Thagard, John Fabian, Frederick Hauck; 6 days 2 hours.

JUNE 27 — *SOYUZ T-9 (USSR)* Manned spacecraft; docked with *Salyut 7;* conducted experiments to control large manned complexes in space; V. Lyakhov, A. Aleksandrov; 149 days 9 hours.

AUG. 30 — *STS-8 (USA)* Third orbital test flight of space shuttle *Challenger;* first night launching of a shuttle; deployed combination weather-communication satellite; Richard Truly, Daniel Brandenstein, William Thornton, Guion Bluford Jr., Dale Gardner; 6 days 1 hour.

OCT. 20 — *PROGRESS 18 (USSR)* Unmanned expendable transport craft; resupplied *Salyut 7.*

NOV. 28 — *STS-9 (USA)* Sixth flight of space shuttle *Columbia;* carried European-built spacelab into orbit to conduct experiments in physics, astronomy and medicine; John Young, Brewster Shaw Jr., Owen Garriott, Ulf Merbold (West Germany), Byron Lichtenberg; 10 days 7 hours.

1984

FEB. 3 — *STS 41-B (USA)* Fourth flight of space shuttle *Challenger;* first untethered space walk; Vance Brand, Robert Gibson, Ronald McNair, Bruce McCandless, Robert Stewart; 7 days 23 hours.

FEB. 8 — *SOYUZ T-10 (USSR)* Manned spacecraft; docked with *Salyut 7;* L. Kizim, V. Solovyov, O. Atkov; 237 days.

APR. 3 — *SOYUZ T-11 (USSR)* Manned spacecraft; international crew; docked with *Salyut 7* (occupied by crew of *Soyuz T-10);* Y. Malyshev, R. Sharma (India), G. Strekalov; 8 days.

APR. 6 — *STS 41-C (USA)* Fifth mission of space shuttle *Challenger;* first repair in space of a damaged satellite, the Solar Maximum, or Solar Max; Robert Crippen, Francis Scobee, George Nelson, Terry Hart, James Van Hoften; 6 days 23 hours.

JULY 17 — *SOYUZ T-12 (USSR)* Docked with *Salyut 7* (still occupied by crew of *Soyuz T-10);* first woman to walk in space; Svetlana Savitskaya (performed 3 hours 30 minutes of EVA), V. Dzhanibekov, I. Volk; 11 days 19 hours.

AUG. 30 — *STS 41-D (USA)* Maiden flight of the space shuttle *Discovery;* deployed three satellites and one experimental solar-power panel; Henry Hartsfield, Michael Coats, Richard Mullane, Judith Resnik, Steven Hawley, Charles D. Walker; 6 days 56 minutes.

OCT. 5 — *STS 41-G (USA)* Sixth flight of the space shuttle *Challenger;* international crew; carried out oceanographic, geologic and meteorologic observations; launched one satellite; Robert Crippen, Jon McBride, Kathryn Sullivan (first EVA by U.S. woman astronaut), Sally Ride, Marc Garneau (Canada), David Leestma, Paul Scully-Power; 8 days 5 hours.

NOV. 8 — *STS 51-A (USA)* Second flight of the space shuttle *Discovery;* first recovery of damaged satellites; Frederick Hauck, David Walker, Anna Fisher, Joseph Allen, Dale Gardner; 7 days 23 hours.

DEC. 15 — *VEGA 1 (USSR)* Probe to Venus and Halley's Comet; reached Venus June 10, 1985; deployed lander/atmospheric balloon; rendezvoused with Halley's Comet on March 6, 1986.

DEC. 21 — *VEGA 2 (USSR)* Probe to Venus and Halley's Comet; reached Venus June 14, 1985; deployed lander/atmospheric balloon; rendezvoused with Halley's Comet on March 9, 1986.

1985

JAN. 7 — *SAKIGAKE (JAPAN)* Unmanned spacecraft; rendezvoused with Halley's Comet in March 1986.

JAN. 24 — *STS 51-C (USA)* Third flight of space shuttle *Discovery;* deployed military satellite; Thomas Mattingly, Loren Shriver, James Buchli, Ellison Onizuka, Gary Payton; 3 days 1 hour.

APR. 12 — *STS 51-D (USA)* Fourth flight of space shuttle *Discovery;* deployed two communications satellites; Karol Bobko, Donald Williams, Charles Walker, Jeffery Hoffman, S. David Griggs, Rhea Seddon, Sen. Jake Garn (R-Utah); 6 days 23 hours.

APR. 29 — *STS 51-B (USA)* Seventh flight of space shuttle *Challenger;* deployed a satellite designed to calibrate radar of air-traffic control centers in North and South America; Robert Overmyer, Frederick Gregory, Don Lind, Taylor Wang, Lodewijk van den Berg, Norman Thagard, William Thornton; 7 days 9 minutes.

JUNE 6 — *SOYUZ T-13 (USSR)* Docked with and revived inert *Salyut 7;* V. Dzhanibekov, V. Savinykh; first crew rotation in space (*T-13* returned to Earth on September 25 with Dzhanibekov and *Soyuz T-14* crew member G. Grechko, who had arrived September 18); 111 days.

JUNE 17 — *STS 51-G (USA)* Fifth flight of space shuttle *Discovery;* international crew; launched three communications satellites; launched and recovered an astronomical research platform; John Creighton, Shannon Lucid, Steven Nagel, Daniel Brandenstein, John Fabian, Prince Sultan Salman Abdel Aziz Al-Saud (Saudi Arabia), Patrick Baudry; 7 days 1 hour.

JULY 2 — *GIOTTO (EUROPEAN SPACE AGENCY)* Unmanned probe; rendezvoused with Halley's Comet on March 13, 1986.

JULY 29 *STS 51-F (USA)* Eighth flight of the space shuttle *Challenger;* carried Spacelab 2 instruments for solar and stellar observation; Gordon Fullerton, Roy Bridges Jr., Anthony England, F. Story Musgrave, Karl Henize, Loren Acton, John-David Bartoe; 7 days 22 hours.

AUG. 27 — *STS 51-I (USA)* Sixth flight of space shuttle *Discovery;* two crew members repaired a satellite in orbit over 2 days of EVA; Joe Engle, Richard Covey, James Van Hoften, William Fisher, John Lounge; 7 days 2 hours.

SEPT. 17 — *SOYUZ T-14 (USSR)* Docked with *Salyut 7* (occupied by crew of *Soyuz T-13*); Vasyutin, A. Volkov, G. Grechko. On September 25, a medical emergency required Grechko and *T-13* crew member V. Dzhanibekov to return to Earth.

OCT. 3 — *STS 51-J (USA)* First flight of the space shuttle *Atlantis;* deployed military payload; Karol Bobko, Ronald Grabe, David Hilmers, William Pailes, Robert Stewart; 4 days 1 hour.

OCT. 30 — *STS 61-A (USA)* Ninth flight of the space shuttle *Challenger;* managed by West Germany, conducted experiments that were developed by a variety of European scientists; Henry Hartsfield, Steven Nagel, Bonnie Dunbar, James Buchli, Guion Bluford Jr., Wubbo Ockels, Ernst Messer-schmid, Reinhard Furrer; 7 days 45 minutes.

NOV. 26 — *STS 61-B (USA)* Second flight of space shuttle *Atlantis;* during more than 12 hours of EVA, two astronauts practiced construction techniques in and around the cargo bay; launched three communications satellites; Brewster Shaw Jr., Bryan O'Connor, Jerry Ross, Sherwood Spring, Mary Cleave, Charles Walker, Rudolfo Neri Vela (Mexico); 6 days 20 hours.

1986

JAN. 12 — *STS 61-C (USA)* Seventh flight of space shuttle *Columbia;* launch postponed a record seven times; deployed a communications satellite and conducted a variety of scientific experiments; was to observe Halley's Comet, but camera failed; Robert Gibson, Charles Bolden, George Nelson, Steven Hawley, Robert Cenker, Franklin Chang-Diaz, Rep. Bill Nelson (D-Fla.); 6 days.

JAN. 28 — *STS 51-L (USA)* Tenth flight of the shuttle *Challenger;* exploded shortly after takeoff, killing all seven crew members aboard; Frances Scobee, Michael Smith, Judith Resnik, Ronald McNair, Ellison Onizuka, Gregory Jarvis, Sharon Christa McAuliffe.

FEB. 20 — *MIR (USSR)* Second space station launched by the Soviet Union; designed with six docking ports for manned and transport spacecraft (*Salyut 7* has two).

MAR. 13 — *SOYUZ T-15 (USSR)* Manned spacecraft; docked with *Mir;* first transfer from one orbiting space station to another, from *Mir* to *Salyut 7;* L. Kizim, V. Solovyov; 125 days.

Glossary

Accelerometer: a device that measures the rate at which speed changes.

Actuator: a device that converts electrical, hydraulic or pneumatic energy into motion.

Algorithm: a step-by-step procedure for solving a problem.

Analog circuit: an electrical path that carries current in a continuously varying form.

Analog computer: a computer in which continuous physical variables, such as the movement of gears or the magnitude of voltage, represent data.

Artificial intelligence (AI): computer programs that emulate such human abilities as learning, perception and reasoning.

Attitude: the orientation of a vehicle (an airplane or a spacecraft, for example), determined by the relationship between a fixed reference line and the craft's longitudinal, lateral and vertical axes.

Axis: any of three fixed lines of reference in an airplane or spacecraft. The labels x, y and z usually refer to the longitudinal, lateral and vertical axes, respectively.

Backup: a hardware component or software program designed to take over for a failed primary device or program. The backup may not necessarily be able to perform every function of a primary system; it serves as a safety measure.

Bit: the smallest unit of information in a computer, represented by a single zero or one. The word "bit" is a contraction of "binary digit."

Buffer: a space reserved in a computer's memory for temporarily storing data, often just before it is to be transmitted or just after it has been received.

Bus: a conductor or set of conductors that transmits information between parts of a computer.

Byte: a sequence of bits, usually eight, treated as a unit for computation or storage.

Center of gravity: the point at which the entire weight of a body is considered concentrated. If supported at this point, the body will remain in equilibrium.

Central processing unit (CPU): the part of a computer that interprets and executes instructions. It is composed of an arithmetic logic unit, a control unit and a small amount of memory.

Color enhancement: the technique of extracting as much information as possible from digital images by exaggerating small differences in color.

Computer language: a set of words, letters, numerals and abbreviated mnemonics, regulated by a specific syntax and used for writing a computer program.

Computer program: a sequence of detailed instructions for performing an operation or solving a problem by computer.

Computer redundancy: a system to protect against hardware failure by employing two or more identical computers to process identical software simultaneously. In cases of triple or quadruple redundancy, the computers may be able to compare data and results to identify a faulty computer.

Computer synchronization: a software procedure used to ensure that redundant computers executing identical software are in step with one another.

Contrast enhancement: the techniques of revealing greater detail in digital-image data by exaggerating minute differences in shading.

Control system: the computerized system in a spacecraft or launch vehicle that executes maneuvers to orient the craft in response to instructions from the guidance system.

Core memory: a type of computer memory that employs thousands of doughnut-shaped, magnetized cores to store one bit apiece. The cores are threaded with wires; pulses travel along the wires to read or record data.

Core-rope memory: a specific type of read-only core memory, in which a wire connected to a magnetized core represents a one, and a disconnected core a zero.

Data compression: a method to reduce the number of bits needed to transmit a given message in the least amount of time.

Digital computer: a machine that operates on data expressed in discrete, or on-off, form rather than the continuous representation used in an analog computer.

Direct sensing: scientific data collected through instruments, such as magnetometers and particle detectors, that come into contact with the immediate atmosphere or environment. *See also* Remote sensing.

Ecliptic plane: the plane of the path traveled by Earth in its annual revolution around the sun.

Equations of motion: the series of mathematical equations that express the position of a body in space as a function of time.

EVA (extravehicular activity): activity by an astronaut that takes place outside the craft, in the vacuum of space; sometimes called a space walk.

Fixed memory: memory that cannot be overwritten, only read.

Frequency: the number of times per second that a wave cycle (one peak and one trough) repeats.

Geostationary: pertains to an orbit 22,300 miles above the equator where, to an observer on Earth, a satellite appears to be stationary because the period of the orbit is exactly 24 hours.

Guidance: the maneuvering sequence required to get an aeronautical or space vehicle from one point to another along a chosen path.

High-gain antenna: an antenna that transmits and receives information via high-frequency electromagnetic waves.

Image processing: computer techniques for creating or reassembling images from digitized data.

Inertial guidance system: self-contained instrumentation that senses a craft's attitude and acceleration, then calculates the vehicle's position and velocity.

Input: information fed into a computer, or from one part of a computer system to another.

Integrated circuit: an electronic circuit whose components are formed on a single piece of semiconductor material (a substance, such as silicon, whose conductivity falls between that of a metal and an insulator).

Interrupt: a temporary halt in executing a program, or a signal causing such a halt.

Launch window: a specific interval during which a spacecraft must be launched to meet its mission goals; frequently used in reference to intercepting a particular orbit around Earth.

Mainframe computer: a large computer typically used to support many users via peripheral devices.

Memory: the storage facilities of a computer. The term usually applies to internal storage as opposed to such external storage as disks or tapes.

Microprocessor: a small computer, with arithmetic and logic functions, that is constructed of integrated circuits, frequently on one chip. Microprocessors are often designed for one purpose, such as running a digital watch.

Modulation: the process of encoding one signal with information contained in another signal.

Multiplexer/demultiplexer (MDM): a device for managing a data bus that sends many transmissions over the same line. On the space shuttle, an MDM encodes incoming sensor data into digital form and sends it on data buses to the shuttle's computers. It also translates digital commands from the computers into analog signals for routing to actuators.

Orbit: the path a satellite takes around a primary body in response to that body's gravitational pull.

Output: the data presented by a computer either directly to the user, to another computer or to some form of storage.

Parallel: refers to the handling of data or instructions in groups of several bits at a time rather than one bit at a time.

Pitch motion: the movement of a craft about its lateral axis; the nose pitches up or down about this axis.

Platforms: large, satellite-like structures designed to orbit near a manned space station and to be used as Earth-observation facilities, astrophysics observatories and zero-gravity laboratories.

Polar orbit: an orbit whose plane passes through Earth's North and South poles.

Random-access memory (RAM): temporary internal memory containing information that can be altered by the CPU; sometimes called read-and-write memory.

Rate gyro: a device that senses the rate of change in a spacecraft's position about its three directional axes of motion.

Read-only memory (ROM): permanent internal memory containing data or operation instructions that cannot be altered.

Real time: pertains to computation that is synchronized with a physical process in the real world.

Remote sensing: scientific data collected through long-range instruments such as radar and cameras.

Retrorocket: a small rocket engine that brakes a space vehicle's forward motion by producing thrust in the opposite direction.

Roll motion: the movement of a craft about its longitudinal axis.

Sensor: an information pickup device that converts physical energy such as temperature into an electrical signal, which may then be translated for use by the computer.

Sequencer: an electronic timing device, used to initiate activities on unmanned probes (for example, before the advent of on-board computers).

Simulator: a facility that uses computers and special equipment to mimic real conditions for the purpose of training crews or testing hardware.

Software: instructions, or programs, designed to be carried out by a computer.

Synthetic-aperture radar (SAR): an imaging system that permits a spacecraft with a relatively small antenna to collect data as if it had a large antenna. The antenna transmits microwave pulses to a planetary surface and collects their reflected echoes as the spacecraft moves along its path.

Telemetry: signals of measured quantities, usually transmitted between a space vehicle and a distant ground station.

Trajectory: a path, followed by a moving body, that has specific beginning and end points.

Transistor: an electronic semiconductor device used as a switch or an amplifier.

Vacuum tube: the earliest form of electronic switch; it was eventually replaced by the transistor.

Word: the basic storage unit of a computer's operation; a sequence of bits — commonly from eight to 32 — occupying a single storage location and processed as a unit by the computer.

Yaw motion: the movement of a craft about its vertical axis; the nose and tail move from side to side.

Bibliography

Books

Baker, David, *The History of Manned Space Flight*. New York: Crown Publishers, 1981.

Battin, Richard H., *Astronautical Guidance*. New York: McGraw-Hill, 1965.

Benson, Charles D., and William Barnaby Faherty, *Moonport: A History of Apollo Launch Facilities and Operations*. Washington, D.C.: NASA, 1978.

Bilstein, Roger E., *Stages to Saturn*. Washington, D.C.: NASA, 1980.

Brooks, Courtney G., James M. Grimwood and Loyd S. Swenson Jr., *Chariots for Apollo: A History of Manned Lunar Spacecraft*. Washington, D.C.: NASA, 1979.

Chubb, W. B., et al., *Flight Performance of Skylab Attitude and Pointing Control System*. Washington, D.C.: NASA, 1975.

Compton, W. David, and Charles D. Benson, *Living and Working in Space*. Washington, D.C.: NASA, 1983.

Corliss, William R., *Histories of the Space Tracking and Data Acquisition Network (STADAN), The Manned Space Flight Network (MSFN), and the NASA Communications Network (NASCOM)*. Washington, D.C.: NASA, 1974.

Dillman, Dennis, *Payload Assist Module (PAM) Deployment Training Manual*. Houston: NASA, 1985.

Dornberger, Walter, *V-2*. New York: The Viking Press, 1954.

Earth Observing System: Data and Information System Report of the EOS Data Panel. Vol. 2a. Greenbelt, Md.: NASA, 1986.

Earth Observing System: Working Group Report. Vol. 1. Greenbelt, Md.: NASA, 1984.

Earth System Science: Overview. Washington, D.C.: Earth System Sciences Committee, NASA Advisory Council, 1986.

The Encyclopedia Americana. Vol. 25. Danbury, Conn.: Grolier, 1986.

Frazier, Kendrick, and the Editors of Time-Life Books, *The Solar System* (Planet Earth series). Alexandria, Va.: Time-Life Books, 1985.

Gatland, Kenneth William, *The Illustrated Encyclopedia of Space Technology*. New York: Crown Publishers, 1981.

Glaese, John R., and Hans F. Kennel, *Low Drag Attitude Control for Skylab Orbital Lifetime Extension*. Washington, D.C.: NASA, 1981.

Glasstone, Samuel, *Sourcebook on the Space Sciences*. Princeton, N.J.: D. Van Nostrand Co., 1965.

Grimwood, James M., *Project Mercury: A Chronology*. Washington, D.C.: NASA, 1963.

Grimwood, James M., and Barton C. Hacker, with P. J. Vorzimmer, *Project Gemini: Technology and Operations*. Washington, D.C.: NASA, 1969.

Hacker, Barton C., and James M. Grimwood, *On the Shoulders of Titans: A History of Project Gemini*. Washington, D.C.: NASA, 1977.

Hall, Eldon C., *Reliability History of the Apollo Guidance Computer*. Cambridge: The M.I.T. Press, 1972.

Introduction to Shuttle Mission Simulation. Houston: NASA, 1983.

Koppes, Clayton R., *JPL and the American Space Program.* New Haven: Yale University Press, 1982.

Lamar, David, et al., *Payload Assist Module System Familiarization Manual.* Houston: NASA, 1986.

Life in Space, by the Editors of Time-Life Books. Alexandria, Va.: Time-Life Books, 1983.

McDougall, Walter A., *The Heavens and the Earth.* New York: Basic Books, 1985.

The McGraw-Hill Encyclopedia of Space. New York: McGraw-Hill, 1968.

Mariner-Mars 1969. Washington, D.C.: NASA, 1969.

Morrison, David, *Voyages to Saturn.* Washington, D.C.: NASA, 1982.

Morrison, David, and Jane Samz, *Voyage to Jupiter.* Washington, D.C.: NASA, 1980.

The New Encyclopaedia Britannica. Vol. 11. Chicago: Helen Hemingway Benton, 1974.

Nicks, Oran W., *Far Travelers: The Exploring Machines.* Washington, D.C.: NASA, 1985.

Osman, Tony, *Space History.* New York: St. Martin's Press, 1983.

Regan, Thomas J., *Shuttle Mission Simulator Instructor Station Console Familiarization Manual.* Houston: NASA, 1985.

Ridpath, Ian, ed., *The Illustrated Encyclopedia of Astronomy and Space.* New York: Thomas Y. Crowell, 1979.

Shore, John, *The Sachertorte Algorithm and Other Antidotes to Computer Anxiety.* New York: Penguin Books, 1985.

Simpson, Theodore R., ed., *The Space Station: An Idea Whose Time Has Come.* New York: IEEE Press, 1985.

Stearns, Edward V. B., *Navigation and Guidance in Space.* Englewood Cliffs, N.J.: Prentice-Hall, 1963.

Stockton, William, and John Noble Wilford, *Space-Liner.* New York: Times Books, 1981.

Swenson, Byron L., Steven W. Squyres and Tony Knight, *A Proposed Comet Nucleus Penetration for the Comet Rendezvous Asteroid Flyby Mission.* New York: Pergamon Press, 1986.

Swenson, Loyd S., Jr., James M. Grimwood and Charles C. Alexander, *This New Ocean: A History of Project Mercury.* Washington, D.C.: NASA, 1966.

Tomayko, James E., *Computers in Space: The NASA Experience.* New York: Marcel Dekker, 1987.

Von Braun, Wernher, and Frederick I. Ordway III, *History of Rocketry & Space Travel.* New York: Thomas Y. Crowell, 1975.

Woodling, C. H., et al., *Apollo Experience Report: Simulation of Manned Space Flight for Crew Training.* Houston: NASA, 1972.

Periodicals

Alonso, Ramon L., and Glenn C. Randa, "Flight-Computer Hardware Trends." *Astronautics & Aeronautics,* Apr. 1967.

Armstrong, Neil, and David Scott, "A Case of 'Constructive Alarm.' " *Life,* Apr. 8, 1966.

"Aurora 7, Do You Read Me?" *Time,* June 1, 1962.

Battin, Richard H., "Space Guidance Evolution: A Personal Narrative." *Journal of Guidance and Control,* Mar./Apr. 1982.

Canby, Thomas Y., "Skylab: Outpost on the Frontier of Space." *National Geographic,* Oct. 1974.

Carlow, Gene D., "Architecture of the Space Shuttle Primary Avionics Software System." *Communications of the ACM,* Sept. 1984.

Carpenter, Scott, "I Got Let In on the Great Secret." *Life,* May 18, 1962.

Casani, J. R., A. G. Conrad and R. A. Neilson, "Mariner 4: A Point of Departure." *Astronautics & Aeronautics,* Aug. 1965.

"Closing the Gap." *Time,* June 11, 1965.

Cooper, A. E., and W. T. Chow, "Development of On-Board Space Computer Systems." *IBM Journal of Research and Development,* Jan. 1976.

Covault, Craig, "Columbia Ready for First Flight." *Aviation Week & Space Technology,* Apr. 6, 1981.

Covault, Craig, and Theresa M. Foley, "NASA Station Design Focuses on Assembly, Early Activation." *Aviation Week & Space Technology,* Sept. 22, 1986.

"Drama from the Moon." *Time,* Apr. 2, 1965.

Draper, Charles S., "Comments." *The Computer Museum Report,* fall 1982.

Edgar, Robert, "On-Board Computers for the Shuttle." *Spaceflight,* Oct. 1975.

Elachi, Charles, "Radar Images of the Earth from Space." *Scientific American,* Dec. 1982.

"The Emerging Face of the Moon." *Time,* Aug. 8, 1969.

"Far-Out Date." *Time,* Dec. 10, 1965.

Feldman, Gene C., "Variability of the Productive Habitat in the Eastern Equatorial Pacific." *EOS Transactions,* Mar. 4, 1986.

Fraser, Donald C., and Philip G. Felleman, "Digital Fly-by-Wire." *Astronautics & Aeronautics,* July/Aug. 1974.

"Gemini's Electronic 'Firsts.' " *Electronics,* May 1965.

"Gemini's Wild Ride." *Time,* Mar. 25, 1966.

"A Giant Leap for Mankind." *Time,* July 25, 1969.

Gore, Rick:

"Sifting for Life in the Sands of Mars." *National Geographic,* Jan. 1977.

"What Voyager Saw: Jupiter's Dazzling Realm." *National Geographic,* Jan. 1980.

"When the Space Shuttle Finally Flies." *National Geographic,* Mar. 1981.

"Guidance Software Programing Advance." *Aviation Week & Space Technology,* Nov. 8, 1976.

Haeussermann, Walter, "Developments in the Field of Automatic Guidance and Control of Rockets." *Journal of Guidance and Control,* May/June 1981.

Hall, Eldon C., "A Designer's View." *The Computer Museum Report,* fall 1982.

Hoag, David G., "The History of Apollo Onboard Guidance, Navigation, and Control." *Journal of Guidance and Control,* Jan./Feb. 1983.

Hooke, Adrian J., "The 1973 Mariner Mission to Venus and Mercury." *Spaceflight,* Dec. 1973.

Hopkins, Albert L., "Electronic Navigator Charts Man's Path to the Moon." *Electronics,* Jan. 9, 1967.

James, S. E., "Evolution of Real-Time Computer Systems for Manned Spaceflight." *IBM Journal of Research Development,* Sept. 1981.

Joyce, Edward J., "The Art of Space Software." *Datamation,* Nov. 15, 1985.

Karp, Harry K., "NASA Plans Global Range to Track Man in Space." *Control Engineering,* July 1959.

Kranz, Eugene F., and James Otis Covington, "Flight Control in the Apollo Program." *Astronautics & Aeronautics,* Mar. 1970.

Laeser, Richard P., William I. McLaughlin and Donna M. Wolff, "Engineering Voyager 2's Encounter with Uranus." *Scientific American,* Nov. 1986.

"The Lessons of Gemini 8." *Time,* Apr. 1, 1966.

Long, Michael E.:

"Magnetic Tape Memory Stores More Data in Space." *Product Engineering,* Apr. 25, 1966.

"Nab's Triumphant Return." *Time,* Feb. 15, 1971.

"Spacelab." *National Geographic,* Sept. 1983.

Martin, Frederick H., and Richard H. Battin, "Computer-Controlled Steering of the Apollo Spacecraft." *Journal of Spacecraft and Rockets,* 1968.

Melbourne, William G., "Navigation between the Planets." *Scientific American,* June 1976.

Morrison, David, and Noel W. Hinners, "A Program for Planetary Exploration." *Science,* May 6, 1983.

North, Warren J., and C. H. Woodling, "Apollo Crew Procedures, Simulation, and Flight Planning." *Astronautics & Aeronautics,* Mar. 1970.

Overbye, Dennis, "Voyager Was on Target Again." *Discover,* Apr. 1986.

Schirra, Walter, and Thomas Stafford, "Astronauts' Own Reports from Gemini 6 and 7." *Life,* Jan. 14, 1966.

Scott, David, "A User's View." *The Computer Museum Report,* fall 1982.

Spector, Alfred, and David Gifford, "The Space Shuttle Primary Computer System." *Communications of the ACM,* Sept. 1984.

"To Fra Mauro and Beyond." *Time,* Feb. 1, 1971.

Tomayko, James E.:

"Achieving Reliability: The Evolution of Redundancy in American Manned Spacecraft Computers." *Journal of the British Interplanetary Society,* 1985.

"Digital Fly-by-Wire." *Aerospace Historian,* Mar. 1986.

"Helmut Hoelzer's Fully Electronic Analog Computer." *Annals of the History of Computing,* July 1985.

"NASA's Manned Spacecraft Computers." *Annals of the History of Computing,* Jan. 1985.

"Toward the Moon." *Time,* June 18, 1965.

"Velocity, Altitude Regimes to Push Computer Limits." *Aviation Week & Space Technology,* Apr. 6, 1981.

"Voyager 2 at Uranus." *The Planetary Report,* Nov./Dec. 1986.

Weiss, E. H., "Tracking Earth Satellites." *Byte,* July 1985.

Wolfe, Thomas, "Columbia's Landing." *National Geographic,* Oct. 1981.

Other Sources

Benson, Tandi, *Payload Deployment and Retrieval System Video Text,* PDRS 2103. NASA, Houston, 1983.

Brown, Charles D., "The Magellan Spacecraft: Its Design, Mission and Challenges." Paper presented at IEEE Eascon 86, Washington, D.C., Sept. 8-10, 1986.

Carley, R. R., C. D. Babb and J. H. Slavin, "Inertial Guidance System Performance Review: Gemini 7/6 Mission." Paper presented at the National Aerospace Electronics Conference, Dayton, May 17, 1966.

Dallas, S. S., and Neal S. Nickle, "The Magellan Mission to Venus." NASA Jet Propulsion Laboratory, California Institute of Technology, n.d.

Dickey, Frederick J., "The 7th Astronaut." Paper presented at conference, Artificial Intelligence from Outer Space . . . Down to Earth. University of Alabama, Huntsville, Oct. 15-16, 1985.

Faget, Maxime A., "The Space Shuttle." NASA, Houston, n.d.

Heacock, Raymond L., "The Voyager Spacecraft." *The Institution of Mechanical Engineers Proceedings, 1980.* Vol. 194.

Laeser, Richard P., "Engineering the Voyager Uranus Mission." Paper presented at IEEE Eascon 86, Washington, D.C., Sept. 8-10, 1986.

LaRussa, Joseph, "Notes on Visual Display Systems." Farrand Optical Co., Valhalla, N.Y., 1980.

McLaughlin, W. I., and D. M. Wolff, "Voyager Flight Engineering: Preparing for Uranus." Paper presented at the AIAA 23rd Aerospace Sciences Meeting, Reno, Nev., Jan. 14-17, 1985.

"Magellan: Venus Radar Mapper." *JPL Fact Sheet.* NASA Jet Propulsion Laboratory, California Institute of Technology, Mar. 1986.

"On-Board Data Processing Technology in the New Generation of Piloted Spaceflight." *Space Transportation System Briefing Series.* NASA Johnson Space Center, Sept. 24, 1980.

Paine, Thomas O., "Leo, Luna and Mars." Paper presented at the NASA Symposium on Lunar Bases and Space Activities of the 21st Century, National Academy of Sciences, Washington, D.C., Oct. 29-31, 1984.

"Project Galileo." *JPL Fact Sheet,* NASA Jet Propulsion Laboratory, California Institute of Technology, Sept. 1985.

"Project Galileo Mission and Spacecraft Design." Paper presented at the AIAA 21st Aerospace Sciences Meeting, Reno, Nev., Jan. 10-13, 1983.

"Report to the President." Presidential Commission on the Space Shuttle Challenger Accident, Washington, D.C., June 6, 1986.

Space Shuttle News Reference. NASA, Houston, n.d.

Space Shuttle Spacecraft Systems. NASA, Houston, n.d.

Voyager 1986 Press Kit. NASA, Washington, D.C., Jan., 1986.

"The Voyager Uranus Travel Guide." NASA Jet Propulsion Laboratory, California Institute of Technology, Aug. 1985.

Yermack, Larry P., "The Space Station: Work Package 3." RCA Astro Electronics Division, Princeton, N.J., May 1986.

Picture Credits

Acknowledgments

The index for this book was prepared by Mel Ingber. The editors also wish to thank: **In France:** Velizy — Louis Moussy, CIMSA. **In the Netherlands:** Hengelo — Hollandse Signaalapparaten B.V.; Schiphol — Fokker Space Division. **In the United States:** Alabama — Huntsville: William Chubb, NASA Marshall Space Flight Center; Helmut Hoelzer; Ludie Richard; Arizona — Tucson: William Boynton, University of Arizona; California — Anaheim: James A. McDivitt, Rockwell International; Downey: Bob Howard and Paul D. Liles, Rockwell International; El Segundo: Kelly McDowell; Moffett Field: Benny Chin and Charles Sobeck, NASA Ames Research Center; Pasadena: Phil Allin, Charles Avis, John Gerpheide, Ray Heacock, Neil Herman, Richard Laeser, Mary Beth Murrill, Neal Nickle and Richard Rice, Jet Propulsion Laboratory; Rancho de Santa Fe: Walter Schirra; Santa Monica: Algirdas Avizienis; Delaware — Newark: Norman F. Ness, University of Delaware; Florida — Merritt Island: Thomas Walton; Maryland — Beltsville: John Morton, Computer Science Corp.; Crofton: Tecwyn Roberts; Gaithersburg: Arnold Levine; Greenbelt: Joseph Dezio, Gene Carl Feldman, Allan Flagg, Velimir Maksimovic and Barbara Walton, NASA Goddard Space Flight Center; Massachusetts — Cambridge: Eldon C. Hall, Charles Stark Draper Laboratory; Ron Kole and Fred Martin, Intermetrics, Inc.; New York — Binghamton: Michael DeAngelis, Singer Link Flight Simulation Division; Valhalla: Joseph LaRussa, Farrand Optical Co., Inc.; Pennsylvania — Sayre: John J. Lenz; Texas — Houston: J. Hundley, IBM Federal Systems Division; Richard P. Parten, Lockheed Engineering and Management Services Company; John R. Garman, Huey Hernandez, Gene McSwain, Barbara Schwartz and John Young, NASA Johnson Space Center; Nora G. Williams, System Development Corp.; Virginia — Arlington: Bill Tindall.

Index

Time-Life Books Inc.
is a wholly owned subsidiary of
TIME INCORPORATED

FOUNDER: Henry R. Luce 1898-1967

Editor-in-Chief: Henry Anatole Grunwald
Chairman and Chief Executive Officer: J. Richard Munro
President and Chief Operating Officer: N. J. Nicholas Jr.
Chairman of the Executive Committee:
Ralph P. Davidson
Corporate Editor: Ray Cave
Executive Vice President, Books: Kelso F. Sutton
Vice President, Books: George Artandi

TIME-LIFE BOOKS INC.

EDITOR: George Constable
Executive Editor: Ellen Phillips
Director of Design: Louis Klein
Director of Editorial Resources: Phyllis K. Wise
Editorial Board: Russell B. Adams Jr., Thomas H.
Flaherty, Lee Hassig, Donia Ann Steele, Rosalind
Stubenberg, Kit van Tulleken, Henry Woodhead
Director of Photography and Research:
John Conrad Weiser

PRESIDENT: Christopher T. Linen
Chief Operating Officer: John M. Fahey Jr.
Senior Vice Presidents: James L. Mercer,
Leopoldo Toralballa
Vice Presidents: Stephen L. Bair, Ralph J. Cuomo, Neal
Goff, Stephen L. Goldstein, Juanita T. James, Hallett
Johnson III, Carol Kaplan, Susan Maruyama, Robert H.
Smith, Paul R. Stewart, Joseph J. Ward
Director of Production Services: Robert J. Passantino

Editorial Operations
Copy Chief: Diane Ullius
Editorial Operations Manager: Caroline A. Boubin
Production: Celia Beattie
Quality Control: James J. Cox (director)
Library: Louise D. Forstall

Correspondents: Elisabeth Kraemer-Singh (Bonn); Maria
Vincenza Aloisi (Paris); Ann Natanson (Rome). Valuable
assistance was also provided by: Elizabeth Brown and
Christina Lieberman (New York).

Library of Congress Cataloguing in Publication Data
Space.
    (Understanding computers)
    Bibliography: p.
    Includes index
    1. Astronautics — Data processing.   I. Time-Life
Books.   II. Series.
TL1078.S63 1987   004   87-6425
ISBN 0-8094-5716-4
ISBN 0-8094-5717-2

For information about any Time-Life book, please write:
Reader Information
541 North Fairbanks Court
Chicago, Illinois 60611

UNDERSTANDING COMPUTERS

SERIES DIRECTORS: Roberta Conlan and Lee Hassig
Series Administrator: Loretta Britten

Editorial Staff for *Space*
Designer: Ellen Robling
Associate Editors: Susan V. Kelly (pictures),
Lydia Preston, principle, Allan Fallow (text)
Researchers: *Writers:*
Roxie France-Nuriddin   Esther Ferington
Tina S. McDowell   Robert M. S. Somerville
Pamela L. Whitney
Assistant Designer: Sue Deal
Editorial Assistant: Miriam P. Newton
Copy Coordinator: Vilasini Balakrishnan
Picture Coordinator: Renée DeSandies

Special Contributors: Ronald H. Bailey, Marcia
Bartusiak, Ken Croswell, Edward Dolnick, Carol Jean
Howard, Valerie Moolman, Steve Olson, David
Thiemann and M. Mitchell Waldrop (text); Steven
Feldman, Melva Holloman, Suzanne Sorrentino and
Susan Stuck (research).

GENERAL CONSULTANT

James E. Tomayko is an associate professor of the Computer Science Department at Wichita State University, where he teaches courses in the history of computing and technology. He recently completed a four-year study, commissioned by NASA, of the agency's use of computers in space flight.

CONSULTANTS

JACK BOYKIN manages the Avionics Systems Office of the National Space Transportation System at the NASA Johnson Space Center. He has been with the space shuttle program since it began.

MARK K. BRYAN is an instructor with Rockwell Shuttle Operations Co. at the NASA Johnson Space Center. He specializes in training crews to operate the shuttle's manipulator arm.

PAUL CERUZZI is associate curator in the Department of Space Science and Exploration at the National Air and Space Museum, Smithsonian Institution. He is currently researching the use of computers in aerospace applications.

STEWART A. COLLINS specializes in interplanetary spacecraft photography at the Jet Propulsion Laboratory. He has contributed to the early missions to Mars and more recently to Voyager's exploration of the giant outer planets.

EDWARD COPPS was manager of software development for the navigation, guidance and control system for the Project Apollo spacecraft. He is a founder of Intermetrics Inc., where he develops software for real-time applications.

ROBERT FRAMPTON is a member of Boeing Aerospace Corporation's Mission Planning Office staff for the Voyager mission to Uranus and Neptune. He is responsible for ensuring that scientists and engineers meet program objectives.

FRANK E. HUGHES runs the Flight Training Branch at the NASA Johnson Space Center, where he is responsible for all astronaut training, from classroom to flight simulators. He is currently planning the curriculum for astronauts destined for the U.S. space station.

PETER M. KACHMAR is a member of the senior engineering staff at the C. S. Draper Laboratory, Inc., in the guidance and navigation section. Specializing in rendezvous techniques, he has participated in the Apollo, Skylab and space shuttle programs.

R. BRAD PERRY JR. is an engineer and instructor for the Shuttle Mission Simulator Facility at the NASA Johnson Space Center. He specializes in training crews in payload handling and manipulation.

MELVIN L. RICHMOND heads the training division at the NASA Johnson Space Center, where he is responsible for training space shuttle astronauts in data-processing systems, navigation systems and rendezvous.

DONNA M. WOLFF, formerly deputy manager for the *Voyager 2* mission, is supervisor of the Mission Planning Group at the Jet Propulsion Laboratory. She participated in the design of the Voyager mission and the future Galileo to Jupiter and Ulysses to the sun missions.